A LIFE ABIDING

Waiting Well and Experiencing Abundance in Christ

GWEN SELLERS

A Life Abiding, Waiting Well and Experiencing Abundance in Christ

Copyright © 2025 by Gwendolyn H. Sellers

Publisher Information
Abundantly Abiding Books LLC
Colorado Springs, CO

For more information or to contact the author, please email
AbundantlyAbiding@gmail.com.

ISBN 979-8-9922805-0-0 (softcover)
ISBN 979-8-9922805-1-7 (eBook)

Cover design: Terry Dugan
Cover photo credit: icemanphotos at Adobe Stock
Editorial team: Saraah Ries, Cristina Wright, and Amy Sinnott
Interior design: Ben Wolf, Inc.
Publishing services provided by BelieversBookServices.com
First printing: 2025
Printed in the United States of America

CONTENTS

NOTE FROM THE AUTHOR

It all started on Valentine's Day—February 14, 2023. Of course, "it" started before then, but that's the day we moved my dad into the nursing home. It was also the day I realized I wasn't using my strengths, and that was a huge problem. Thus began a journey of exploration, discovery, renewed passion, and a steadily growing desire to help other women know God, love him, wait faithfully on him, and experience a life of abiding in all its fullness.

Fittingly, one year later on February 15, I was invited to give a devotion on the theme of waiting to a group of women, which prompted thoughts of something more. That "something more" is the book you are holding in your hands today.

Ultimately, this book is an expression of my love for God because of his great love for me. It's also an expression of love for his people. My prayer is that this book will prompt you to know how deeply loved you are by God, to faithfully abide in him by the power of the Holy Spirit, to experience true fullness of life in Christ, and to yearn all the more deeply for final redemption.

Wait for the LORD;
be strong, and let your heart take courage;
wait for the LORD!
PSALM 27:14

INTRODUCTION

Have you ever felt like you were waiting on everything and everyone? That describes my situation in 2023—2024. My dad was nearing the end of his journey with Huntington's disease, and my place of work was going through organizational growing pains. God was stirring my mind and heart, pointing out burnout, reigniting former passions, and clarifying my purpose. I knew change was coming, but I didn't know what it would look like or when it would happen.

To top it all off, it seemed like everywhere I went this theme of waiting kept coming up. My church did a "year of sabbath" in which we intentionally cleared the church calendar every seven weeks, except for an all-church worship night and a unique weekend service. This was to provide space to pause, connect with God in a different way, and connect with one another. The theme of waiting came up in several sermon series throughout the year as well as in podcasts and conversations with others in similar liminal spaces. Then I was asked to talk at a women's group on their yearly theme—resting, trusting, waiting—using Psalm 27:14 as the foundation. Do you think God was communicating something to me?

In his faithfulness, God refined that theme. It wasn't just about waiting, but about *abiding*. That word took on a special significance for me during an activity in a class I was taking. Then, as often seems to be the case, it just kept coming up.

Meanwhile, God was stirring my passion for leadership, design, and abundant life. Seeing my life of waiting within the grander narrative of redemptive history gave it more meaning. I began to see how I was not waiting for a particular end. Rather, life is about abiding in God—faithfully seeking his presence, longing for the fullness of his promises, and living fully present. I wanted to learn how to yearn for the completion of God's plan while being fully present in the ways he was currently working out that plan. In short, I wanted to abide—both in God and in his current plans for me. I wanted to be like the people in Hebrews 11 who lived by faith, hoping for better things, all the while obediently living out their part of God's plan.

This book will not jump too quickly or dive too deeply into talk of abundant life because God is teaching me to linger. To truly abide, we need to truly wait. Yes, this world is filled with goodness. There is abundance in Christ. Living out God's design of us, both by living his ways in general and by stewarding the unique things he has entrusted to us, touches the deepest longings of our hearts. There is rest and filling, even in this in-between as we await eternity. Yet, all too often, I (and perhaps you too) am eager to put a bow on things, to look at the joy without attending to the longings, to think only of completion instead of waiting. It may feel comfortable in the moment, but I'm finding that all it does is diminish our longings and dampen our appreciation of the depth of God's grace. It prompts us to settle for the things of the world as if they are the substance instead of the shadow. So, let's linger in the waiting and do the work of abiding. There is incredible joy in it, but we first need to simply be.

That is my hope for you in reading this book. I would love

to sit down with you over coffee—to hear your story, to know the longings of your heart, to see the unique design God gave you, to share in your grief over the world's brokenness, to rejoice with you in the glimpses of beauty and restoration, to long for final fullness, and to encourage you to confidently live a life of abiding in God. This life matters. *You matter.* God designed you for a purpose and placed you right where you are. He calls you to abide in him and live for him. Yes, it involves deep pain. And, yes, it involves incredible joy! We get to experience all of it, resting in him, waiting for him, and abiding in him as we abide in this life he has entrusted to us.

CHAPTER 1

PREPARATION FOR THE JOURNEY

How are you at waiting? If you're anything like me, not always great. Something as simple as the grocery store reveals this to me. No matter how intellectually certain I am that the self-checkout lane takes longer than a regular lane when I have produce or coupons, I keep using it. For some reason, it just feels better to not wait—that is until I have to wait for the attendant to help me with whatever problem I run into! Am I the only one for whom this struggle is real?

While I could grow in my daily patience, that is not the type of waiting I have in mind when asking the question. I'm thinking more about things like relational reconciliation, physical healing, direction for a new life season, an unsaved loved one to come to know the Lord, deliverance from a challenging circumstance, a longing to be emotionally fulfilled, and even spiritual growth. Really, I'm thinking about eternity. What is it like for you to live in this time of in-between, where Christ has come and yet we await his return, where redemption is real and yet the fullness of God's plans is not yet complete? Do you find your soul longing for something you can't quite describe? We desire so much, but we often find ourselves waiting.

Waiting is hard! It comes with all sorts of emotions and reactions. Perhaps you feel alone, anxious, uncertain, tempted to force things, willing to settle for less, confused, frustrated, or helpless. In contrast, maybe you feel hopeful and excited to see what God will do. Perhaps it's a time when you are so dependent on God that you're feeling spiritually alive and growing. Or maybe you feel all of those things at once. I know I have.

What are we to do with all this waiting? If you read the introduction or even just the title of the book, you know what I think the answer is: abide. If you didn't read the introduction, go back; I'll wait …

So, what is abiding? How is it related to waiting? And why does it matter? This is the journey I'd like you to join me on. It's a journey of discovering God's redemptive plan for all of humanity and how your life fits into it. Really, it's a journey of discovering God, of learning to dwell with him in the present and yearning for the time when "the dwelling place of God is with man. He will dwell with them, and they will be his people, and God himself will be with them as their God" (Revelation 21:3). It's a journey of grief, longing, joy, hopefulness, peace, and even exhilaration.

DEFINITIONS

Before we begin our journey, let's establish a few basics. Every good conversation is built on a foundation of shared understanding. So, let's start with some definitions. When defining words in the Bible, it's useful to look at the original Hebrew and Greek roots.

Wait

Psalm 27:14 is a new favorite verse for me; it's the one that comes to mind when I think about waiting. It says, "Wait for the LORD; be strong, and let your heart take courage; wait for the LORD!" Isn't that so encouraging?

The Hebrew root word for *wait* in this verse is *qâvâh*. Strong's defines it partially with words like "expect, look, patiently, tarry, wait (for, on, upon)."[1] Romans 8:25 uses the Greek root word *apekdéchomai*, which Strong's defines with words like, "to expect fully; look (wait) for."[2]

When we're talking about waiting, we're talking about eager expectation. It requires patience, but it is something we are actively looking for. My nephews are a wonderful illustration of this concept. We have a family vacation about once a year, and it seems like every time I'm with them I learn something about God. One year, at about age five, one of my nephews wanted to put on a show for any of the adults willing to watch. We told him we'd be out in about twenty minutes. He happily ran outside to set up, eager to entertain us, and more than willing to wait. He did not get distracted, nor did he leave his stage until we came. Why would a child wait that long? Because he knew we would be true to our word, and he genuinely wanted to share his skill with us. So, he patiently looked for us to come.

Another time, when another nephew was three, he wanted to go outside to wait for his dad to come home from work. Again, the wait would be about twenty minutes. I was incredulous that a toddler could make it that long, but he sat on the sidewalk, happy as could be, looking for his dad's car to come down the road. Why? Because he knew his dad would come and that he would get a special ride in the car.

---

1. "H6960 - qāvâ - Strong's Hebrew Lexicon (esv)." Blue Letter Bible, accessed March 15, 2024, https://www.blueletterbible.org/lexicon/h6960/esv/wlc/0-1/.

2. "G553 - apekdechomai - Strong's Greek Lexicon (esv)." Blue Letter Bible, accessed March 15, 2024, https://www.blueletterbible.org/lexicon/g553/esv/mgnt/0-1/.

He looked patiently for his dad because he wanted to be with him, and he knew he would come.

This is what I have in mind when talking about waiting on God. We are eagerly looking for him because we know he is true to his word and that he comes. We wait with patience and expectation.

Abide

Psalm 91:1 says, "He who dwells in the shelter of the Most High will abide in the shadow of the Almighty." The Hebrew root word linked to *abide* in this verse is *yâshab*, which Strong's defines, in part, as, "to sit down; by implication, to dwell, to remain; to settle, to marry" and gives words like "abide, continue, dwell, ease self, endure, establish, habitation, haunt, inhabit, remain, return, tarry."[3]

John 15:1–17 is one of my favorite passages, and the word *abide*, from the Greek *ménō,* is prominent. The same word is used numerous times throughout the New Testament. One is in 1 John 2:28, which says, "And now, little children, abide in him, so that when he appears we may have confidence and not shrink from him in shame at his coming." A partial definition from Strong's includes: "to stay (in a given place, state, relation, or expectancy)" and "abide, continue, dwell, endure, be present, remain, stand, tarry."[4]

Abiding can be as simple as inhabiting a certain physical space and as deep as truly dwelling, enduring, and remaining. Jesus' illustration in John 15 is related to a vine and branches. A branch is not merely connected to the vine; it

---

3. "H3427 - yāšaḇ - Strong's Hebrew Lexicon (esv)." Blue Letter Bible, accessed March 15, 2024, https://www.blueletterbible.org/lexicon/h3427/esv/wlc/0-1/.

4. "G3306 - menō - Strong's Greek Lexicon (esv)." Blue Letter Bible, accessed March 15, 2024, https://www.blueletterbible.org/lexicon/g3306/esv/mgnt/0-2/#lexResults.

receives its life from the vine. We abide when we are fully present, intimately linked.

The English definition of *abide* is too good not to share. It includes concepts like bearing patiently, enduring, waiting for, remaining stable, and sojourning.[5] I love the link between abiding and waiting. The idea of "bearing patiently" or "tolerating" makes me laugh. Isn't that what our waiting often feels like?

Abundant Life

In John 10:10 Jesus said, "I came that they may have life and have it abundantly." The word abundantly describes the type of life Jesus gives. It is "over and above, more than is necessary, superadded" or "exceedingly abundantly, supremely."[6] As the author of life, God gives that which is truly life. Jesus isn't talking about just keeping our hearts beating but about us being fully alive as intended. This is about living out our design as image-bearers (Genesis 1:27), living the life-giving ways of God (John 15:10–11; 1 John 5:1–5), and living out our particular purpose in any given season (Psalm 139; 1 Peter 4:10–11).

We will experience the fullness of this abundant life in eternity (Revelation 21—22), but even now we can experience abundant life in Christ. "In him was life, and the life was the light of men" (John 1:4), and he is "the way, and the truth, and the life" (John 14:6). This abundance does not mean lack of hardship; in fact, sometimes living God's way leads directly to suffering (John 16:33; 2 Timothy 3:12). But it does mean living with purpose as active participants in God's

---

5. "abide – Merriam Webster." Merriam-Webster, accessed March 15, 2024, https://www.merriam-webster.com/dictionary/abide.

6. "G4053 - perissos - Strong's Greek Lexicon (esv)." Blue Letter Bible, accessed July 6, 2024, https://www.blueletterbible.org/lexicon/g4053/esv/mgnt/0-1/.

work in the world (Genesis 1:28; 9:7; John 15:12–17; 1 Peter 1:3–25). As we abide in God in the in-between, waiting for completion, we can experience abundance.

Grander redemptive arc

Our understanding of our own lives and of abiding is intricately linked to our recognition of God's redemptive plan for all of humanity. What is this grander redemptive arc of history? It's the incredible journey from Genesis 1 through Revelation 22. It's the reality that God created humanity in his image and for his glory, for relationship with him and with each other, and with purpose in the world (Genesis 1—2). It's the heartbreak of sin (going against God's ways) that led to death and brokenness being an insidious reality in our world (Genesis 3). God promises to provide salvation and his patience in unfolding that plan. It's the old covenant and the new covenant (see the New Testament book of Hebrews). It's Jesus' life, death, and resurrection—his victory over sin and death. It's his promised return to bring final judgment and to make all things new (Revelation 19—22). If you're unfamiliar with this story, or if you just need a refresher, check out the Appendix for more.

We live in the in-between. The promised Savior of the Old Testament has come, and yet we await Jesus' return. Romans 8:23–25 explains, "And not only the creation, but we ourselves, who have the firstfruits of the Spirit, groan inwardly as we wait eagerly for adoption as sons, the redemption of our bodies. For in this hope, we were saved. Now hope that is seen is not hope. For who hopes for what he sees? But if we hope for what we do not see, we wait for it with patience." Second Peter 3:9–11 encourages us, "The Lord is not slow to fulfill his promise as some count slowness, but is patient toward you, not wishing that any should perish, but that all should reach repentance. But the day of the Lord will come like a thief, and then the heavens will pass away with a roar, and the heavenly bodies will be burned up and dissolved, and the earth and the works that are done on it will be exposed. Since all these things are thus to be dissolved, what sort of people ought you to be in lives of holiness and godliness."

When I refer to redemptive history or the grander redemptive arc, this is what I mean. Where do we fit into God's overall plan? How does knowing his work from creation to final restoration affect our lives today? What does this mean for our abiding and waiting? As we'll discover, it makes a huge difference!

THE PATH FOR OUR JOURNEY

With these definitions in place, we're almost set to begin our journey of discovery. The route may feel a bit odd at times, but I'll do my best to provide a linear way forward, even though waiting doesn't always feel linear. There is usually no set end date and often no set destination. Our destination is simply to know, love, and trust God more. I'm going to be offering some thoughts, but how you get there will ultimately be about you and God engaging in this together. I'd suggest you invite some friends along the way too. Even for introverts like me, the journey is usually richer together!

We'll start by getting a solid foundation on waiting as a general concept. Then we'll explore how we can look to the past, yearn for the future, and live in the present, using Psalm 27 as a loose guide. I'll touch on the realities of grief and transition. Then I'll provide some thoughts and practical tips about what it means to abide, using John 15 to guide us. In all of this, we'll do our best to settle in and wait expectantly for what God reveals. May you be encouraged to abide in him and know that whatever the final destination looks like in your life, if you're with him, it will be good!

CHAPTER 2

WAITING—WHAT'S THE POINT?

When someone mentions waiting, what comes to mind? Does it sound like a positive experience? Needed white space? Something to avoid at all costs? An expected inconvenience? The bane of your existence? I think, generally speaking, our society struggles to wait; we don't think of waiting as desirable or see much value in it. In fact, we've become quite adept at designing ways to avoid waiting or ways of entertaining ourselves when waiting is the only option. But what about waiting for the Lord? Is it different?

I've come to learn that when we are waiting for the Lord, looking expectantly to him, and resting in trust, there is goodness. Waiting certainly doesn't always feel good! But this is not a book about how to endure because that's our only option. As hard as it can be sometimes, waiting is not pointless drudgery. No! It's an invitation to abide. And abiding is key to abundant life in Christ. Waiting on God is always worth it!

No doubt you know this truth intuitively, and you probably have a few stories that make the point. Let me share one of mine. Several years ago, I made the move from paying rent to paying mortgage. That decision in itself took a year or so.

But once I decided to make the move, I had what I thought was the perfect plan in mind—what I was looking for and when it would happen, all on my timeline. Unsurprisingly, my timeline did not pan out. In the midst of my anxiety, tinged with a little anger, God kept showing up in the details. During my time of waiting, the owner of my apartment allowed me to continue my lease on a month-to-month basis at the same rate, a friend anonymously gave me a monetary gift that allowed me to be more comfortable about an eventual downpayment, and I came to a better understanding of what type of home I would actually need. When the perfect condo finally became available, my offer was quickly accepted. The place I live now is exactly what I need and feels like home. Throughout that waiting process, God affirmed his faithfulness, and the experience deepened my trust in him. It gave me tangible markers of God's care for me, and I came to recognize that his provision was far greater than my supposedly perfect plan.

Even better, the delay wasn't just about me and my faith. The shifted timeline meant the open house I hosted to welcome friends to my new home was later than it would have been otherwise. Unbeknownst to me when scheduling it, a military friend of mine (who was on an extended assignment overseas) just happened to be home for one week—the week of my open house—and he decided to come. Meanwhile, a college friend of mine decided to invite a mutual friend (whom I'd not seen in years), and she agreed to come. The two unexpected guests hit it off, dated for a year, and are now married with a son. Not only was God deepening my trust in him in the waiting, but he was orchestrating a plan for the lives of others I never could have dreamed up. The wait was well worth it.

What things would you have missed in life if waiting weren't part of it? What would others have missed if waiting weren't part of your story?

BIBLICAL VIEW OF WAITING

It's been said that God's people have always been a waiting people. I think of Noah who waited inside the ark for over a year for the flood waters to recede (Genesis 6—9), Abraham and Sarah who waited at least twenty-five years for the birth of Isaac (Genesis 12—17; 21), the Israelites who waited four hundred years before their rescue from Egypt (Exodus 1—2), Moses waiting forty years in Midian (Exodus 2—4), David who was anointed over ten years before taking the throne (1 Samuel 16), Daniel and the captives in Babylon waiting for the seventy years to be complete before returning home to Jerusalem (Daniel 9:2), and Jesus who did not begin his public ministry until the age of about thirty (Luke 3:23). God is in no rush, and his timing is perfect.

I love how Galatians 4:4 says, "But when the fullness of time had come, God sent forth his son." Jesus came at exactly the right time, and he will return at exactly the right time (Matthew 24:36; 2 Peter 3:9–10). Hebrews 11 gives examples of people who demonstrated faith in God. An interlude in Abraham and Sarah's story explains, "These all died in faith, not having received the things promised, but having seen them and greeted them from afar, and having acknowledged that they were strangers and exiles on the earth. For people who speak thus make it clear that they are seeking a homeland. If they had been thinking of that land from which they had gone out, they would have had opportunity to return. But as it is, they desire a better country, that is, a heavenly one. Therefore God is not ashamed to be called their God, for he has prepared for them a city" (Hebrews 11:13–16). They saw their place in the grander redemptive arc, and it made a difference.

Hebrews 11:39–40 concludes a listing of faithful men and women by saying, "And all these, though commended through their faith, did not receive what was promised, since

God had provided something better for us, that apart from us they should not be made perfect." The people of God wait expectantly because we trust our God. We know something good is planned, and it is worth the wait. We know God's timing is right, so we abide in him in our present circumstances, all the while anticipating the future.

GOD'S PURPOSE IN OUR WAITING

God's timing is not only perfect in the grand scheme of things but in our personal lives. There is purpose in our waiting. Sometimes we see that purpose immediately, like when the outcome of our situation is better because of the time delay. Other times, we may not understand the precise purpose of our waiting, either within the grander narrative or within the narrative of our own lives. Yet, we know God does everything for a purpose, so we cling to the truth of who he is.

Sanctification

A primary purpose of waiting is sanctification. How often is your faith challenged and thereby deepened when you're waiting? Do you have a better understanding of God's heart, hating the realities of brokenness more, and longing even more deeply for the wholeness and restoration God will bring? Does waiting increase your empathy and compassion, and thus your ability to better love others with God's love? What does waiting do to your desires—refine them, change them, clarify them? How about your beliefs? Does it cause you to make sure that what you believe is actually true? Does it make you courageous in your stand for the truth, clinging to the Word of God instead of circumstances? Does waiting cause you to depend more on God? To appreciate community all the more? In my experience, times of waiting can do all of these things, particularly when we intentionally abide in God.

We may not always know the purpose of waiting, but we know God is good and trustworthy. As some have said, "The worst is not the last." When we are in seasons of waiting, perhaps wrestling with the unknown, we draw near to God, abiding in him.

Psalm 131 is a fitting prayer when we wait:

> O LORD, my heart is not lifted up;
> my eyes are not raised too high;
> I do not occupy myself with things
> too great and too marvelous for me.
> But I have calmed and quieted my soul,
> like a weaned child with its mother;
> like a weaned child is my soul within me.
> O Israel, hope in the LORD
> from this time forth and forevermore.

Preparation

Sometimes waiting is preparation—something God shapes in us or others or our circumstances will be important for another life season. Moses' life is one of the best biblical examples of this. Consider how he needed to be educated in Egyptian ways for the first forty years of his life to hold an audience with the pharaoh at a later time. Consider how his forty years as a shepherd in Midian equipped him to lead the Israelites for forty years in the desert. Moses may have felt lost during those forty years, having the desire to rescue his people but seemingly having failed (Exodus 2:11–15, 22; 4:13). Or consider Jesus who spent about thirty years in relative obscurity before beginning his public ministry (Luke 3:23). During that time, he "increased in wisdom and in stature and in favor with God and man" (Luke 2:52). Throughout his public ministry, he was keenly aware of appropriate timing (Luke 9:51; John 2:4).

The in-betweens matter. It's been said that life is not a series of events but a collection of moments. Don't discount the times that feel like a waste; God is building something. You might be able to look back and see the character change God worked out or the needed skills and experience those years of waiting provided. Other times you won't see such a direct link. But we know enough about God to know he does not waste experiences, and his timing is perfect (Romans 8:28–30).

Revelation

Our waiting does not always lead to the expected end. Have you ever been waiting for something specific only to see your desires change in the interim? Sometimes the waiting process is an exploration during which God reveals things in our hearts and lives and gradually shapes and reshapes our desires (Psalm 37:4). As we look expectantly for God and take each next right step, something unexpected unfolds. I experienced this in a burnout situation wherein my proposed solutions led to ends I never would have imagined and were so much better and more complete for all involved. I knew the right next step to take but did not know the final destination. Sometimes our waiting is not about the entirety of the situation but about being faithful in each in-between moment. We might imagine one thing at the start, but as it unfolds, we see God is up to something else. That's a scary thought in many ways, but pretty exhilarating! Waiting requires risk and trust and persistence; to wait well, we must believe God will be who he is—sovereign and good.

The illustration of a trapeze is sometimes used to describe this type of situation. In fact, I was in an in-between in my life when a podcast mentioned the common trope. That was a "love note" from God, as my mom would say, and a confirmation to keep pressing forward. It was a meaningful reminder as I know the thrill of being on a trapeze. The summer after I graduated high school, my family went to a resort in Curaçao that offered a trapeze experience. Strapped into a harness and with a net beneath, I learned to hang from one trapeze bar, flip, let go, and be caught by a professional on the other side. It was incredible! The freedom of flying in mid-air is only paralleled by the freedom I often feel in running. It felt completely safe, so I could be completely free to simply enjoy. Looking at pictures afterward, my mom commented on the way I was truly in mid-air; others kept their legs attached to one trapeze bar until the professional caught them. But I let go, and I'm guessing I had a better experience because of it.

I wonder how much more I would let go in life if I more fully trusted God. In my season of obvious waiting, I became willing to risk more, unsure of the outcome, but certain of the call to stand firm and to move. It only deepened my trust in God. Perhaps because I am a little new to dreaming and risking, God showed me the fruit nearly immediately. That is not to say it was easy or painless, but God was so clearly at work that I cannot imagine what it would have been like to cling to the old instead of moving toward the new. Or maybe it's that, in the waiting, God was teaching me how to be on the lookout for him. Waiting is not about sitting around until things change; it's about looking expectantly. When we ask God to open our eyes, often his presence is unmistakable, and the call becomes clear.

Relationship

Keep in mind that God's call is not always painless or costless, and sometimes we don't see it with clarity. My daily practices on the trapeze were fun and harmless, but the night I got to perform in the circus was another story. In my nervousness, I let go too soon and ended up gouging the professional's arm with my fingernail because of it. Obviously, it's not a perfect comparison, but I share this to say there are times when we act in trust but circumstances seem to get worse. Many of the prophets and apostles could tell you that obeying God came at great personal cost to them. Elijah's despair is unquestionable (1 Kings 19). Other times, we move too soon and much of the mess is our own fault. Abraham, Sarah, and Hagar can tell you what that is like (Genesis 16). And, of course, other people, the general fallen nature of the world, and spiritual warfare are all at play. Our circumstances are generally not solid indicators of whether we are obeying God. But if we are abiding in him and seeking him, we can rest and trust that he will catch us (Romans 8:28–30).

Though our waiting is generally linked to circumstances of some kind, it is not the circumstances that are ultimate. God's work and our relationship with him matter more than any temporal situation. God remains faithful to his people in every circumstance; this is evident throughout the biblical narrative. And he remains faithful to us (Hebrews 13:5–8). We're mid-story, so we don't always understand the full plotline or expect the twists or know the importance of any given situation. God does not always deliver us from suffering or give us an indication of how he will redeem it, but he is with us through it. We are invited to call out to him. We can remind ourselves of the truth of who he is and confidently proclaim his character. We can wrestle with him when we don't understand. We can trust that he is a capable author, writing a good story, and working all the pieces together in ways we cannot fully fathom (Ephesians 3:20–21). All of this —fully engaging in the story of our lives in whatever the current plotline looks like, with an eye toward the author—is part of waiting on God.

God is at work in your waiting. Whether you are gripping one trapeze bar, desperately wishing for the time God says to let go, in mid-air feeling exhilarated (or perhaps terrified), safely caught on the other side, or something seems to have gone awry and you're freefalling, wondering where God is and what the safety net is going to be, you can trust that God sees, he is with you, and he is at work. So, keep abiding!

WHEN WAITING IS NOT GOOD

Waiting for the Lord draws us closer to him; it draws out our trust, develops our character, aligns us with his will and his timing, gives us an opportunity to see and experience things we may not have otherwise, and more. But there is a type of waiting that is not good. Likely, you know this intuitively as well.

The most obvious example is when we're waiting for some circumstantial reality before paying attention to needed character change. Have you ever known someone who is waiting until they aren't busy before they attend to important relationships in their lives? Or what about a single friend who is waiting to get married before moving on to other portions of God's will for his or her life, perhaps not even seeking other portions of his will? Or someone waiting on a spouse to change before they decide to really "get into church"? There are, indeed, seasons in life, and sometimes we really cannot act on something until a circumstance changes. But there are other times when we are blinded by the "tyranny of the urgent" and use waiting as an excuse to neglect the thing we know we're called to.

Perhaps more perniciously, sometimes this happens with dreams. It's one thing when we know we're using waiting as an excuse to merely delay attending to the things God has called us to. We know life won't suddenly become less busy and that if we want to invest in relationships we need to do so now. We know our relationship with God cannot depend on someone else's level of spiritual maturity. We know our marital status is not the totality of our lives. If we took a moment to step back and evaluate, we would realize it is time to act. But what about those times we don't realize we're waiting on circumstantial change to fully live?

I've been in this situation before. My dad was diagnosed with Huntington's disease (a neurodegenerative illness) in 2010, and we had no idea how long the journey would be or what it would look like. As the years progressed, I found myself holding my breath for his death. I'd unintentionally put other things in my life on pause thinking I would soon be engulfed by dealing with his death, needing to grieve, needing to adjust, and then could make changes. This coincided with work burnout, which I consistently excused as just needing a vacation or stress about my parents' situation (my dad was living at home at the time and in need of increasingly more care). Praise God, my mom named my burnout for what it was. God helped me see specific reasons and solutions. He also provided timely support and clarity through connecting with a life coach. Much to my surprise, God gave me the ability to dream! He reignited passions long forgotten, gave me opportunities to work in my gifting, and invigorated me. I had unintentionally stopped paying attention because one thing in my life was clouding my view. Certainly, many other factors were at play, and I believe it all happened in precisely God's timing. But the situation reminded me to not wait to live.

There will never be a perfect time for something from a human perspective, but there is from God's perspective. Don't wait for perfection before you act on what God is calling you to do. Don't wait for something in your life to be a reality before engaging fully in the process of sanctification. Don't wait to have that meaningful conversation or to express your love to others. Don't wait to abide and experience abundance.

CHAPTER 3

REMEMBERING THE PAST

By definition, when we are waiting, we are living between the past and the future. Actually, all of our living occurs in this gap—otherwise known as the present! But when we're waiting, it feels particularly tense, doesn't it? We are keenly aware that where we have been is not where we are, and that we are not yet where we are going. So, how do we abide in this present tension? In my experience, remembering is a helpful first step. What do I mean by that?

First, remember the unchanging truths on which we can hang our proverbial hats. We know what the Bible says about God's attributes and actions. When we cling to the reality of who he is, which is who he always has been and who he always will be, our present feels less nebulous. We know who he is because he has told us, and he has demonstrated it to us. Primarily, this is through the biblical narrative. But it also comes through things like creation, historical church creeds, and systematic theology. Avail yourself of your knowledge of God, and let it serve as a declaration and an anchor when you are unsettled.

But this isn't just about intellectual knowledge. Remembering also means rehearsing our personal histories with God. The God who inspired genealogies to be a part of Scripture—who spoke to Adam, Eve, Abraham, Hagar, Moses, and Elijah, who took on human flesh and dwelt among people, who called men and women to follow him both then and now—is the same God whose Spirit dwells in you if you are in Christ. He's the God who knows you intimately, loves you completely, and is actively at work in your life. God's work did not end with the closing of the biblical canon. You have stories of God's faithfulness in your own life, plus this family history of his faithfulness in the lives of his people for millennia. Call those memories to mind and allow them to encourage you that God still sees you and is still working.

Psalm 27 demonstrates this well. In fact, it also helps us know how to yearn for the future and live in the present. David is the author, and while this psalm is not explicitly linked to a specific event in his life, some think he wrote it while on the run from his son Absalom, who had attempted a coup, or King Saul, who wanted to kill him.

> The LORD is My Light and My Salvation
> Of David.
> The LORD is my light and my salvation;
>   whom shall I fear?
> The LORD is the stronghold of my life;
>   of whom shall I be afraid?
> When evildoers assail me
>   to eat up my flesh,
> my adversaries and foes,
>   it is they who stumble and fall.
> Though an army encamp against me,
>   my heart shall not fear;
> though war arise against me,
>   yet I will be confident.
> One thing have I asked of the LORD,

that will I seek after:
that I may dwell in the house of the LORD
    all the days of my life,
to gaze upon the beauty of the LORD
    and to inquire in his temple.
For he will hide me in his shelter
    in the day of trouble;
he will conceal me under the cover of his tent;
    he will lift me high upon a rock.
And now my head shall be lifted up
    above my enemies all around me,
and I will offer in his tent
    sacrifices with shouts of joy;
I will sing and make melody to the LORD.
Hear, O LORD, when I cry aloud;
    be gracious to me and answer me!
You have said, 'Seek my face.'
My heart says to you,
    'Your face, LORD, do I seek.'
    Hide not your face from me.
Turn not your servant away in anger,
    O you who have been my help.
Cast me not off; forsake me not,
    O God of my salvation!
For my father and my mother have forsaken me,
    but the LORD will take me in.
Teach me your way, O LORD,
    and lead me on a level path
    because of my enemies.
Give me not up to the will of my adversaries;
    for false witnesses have risen against me,
    and they breathe out violence.
I believe that I shall look upon the goodness of the LORD
    in the land of the living!
Wait for the LORD;

> be strong, and let your heart take courage;
> wait for the LORD!

Notice how verses 1 through 3 are filled with affirmations of God's character and rehearsals of things God had done in David's past. Let's take a closer look.

REMEMBERING WHO GOD IS—PSALM 27:1

David begins with a proclamation of who God is. Knowing God is his light, salvation, and stronghold; David boldly states he need not fear. David's confidence is rooted in the reality of God's character. Ours should be too. The Bible tells us who God is, and we can stand strong knowing he does not change. God's immutability is my favorite of his attributes. I can trust he will be the same always and forever (Exodus 3:14; Hebrews 13:8). When I'm unsteady in the waiting, reminding myself of the steadfastness of God and the consistency of his character both go a long way in helping me stand firm.

We find worshipful proclamations of who God is throughout the Bible. For example, in Psalm 18:1–3, David writes:

> I love you, O LORD, my strength.
> The LORD is my rock and my fortress and my deliverer,
>   my God, my rock, in whom I take refuge,
>   my shield, and the horn of my salvation, my stronghold.
> I call upon the LORD, who is worthy to be praised,
>   and I am saved from my enemies.

Ephesians 3:14–21 extols God's love and power. Ephesians 1:3–14 talks about his gifts to those who are in Christ and their security in him. Hebrews 13:5–6 says, "He has said, 'I will never leave you nor forsake you.' So, we can confidently say, 'The Lord is my helper; I will not fear; what can man do to me?'" Romans 8:37–39 tells us, "No, in all these things we are more than conquerors through him who loved us. For I am sure that neither death nor life, nor angels nor rulers, nor things present nor things to come, nor powers, nor height nor depth, nor anything else in all creation, will be able to separate us from the love of God in Christ Jesus our Lord." The psalms are replete with praises of God's character and actions. Like David, we can stand boldly and confidently in God, knowing him in whom we have believed and trusting that he is who he claims to be.

It is not always easy to remind ourselves of the unchanging truths of God while we wait. Doubts begin to creep in, earthly things take our focus, our unmet desires can become consuming, or we might simply be antsy in the delay and tempted to force things on our own. We know removing our focus from God and taking matters into our own hands never ends well. But it's also a genuine struggle for our hearts to believe what we know to be true when our circumstances are shouting to us otherwise. So, what are we to do?

We need to prepare beforehand as well as intentionally and continually refocus our eyes on God. Growth in Christ is something we should always be doing, no matter our current circumstances. We always need to be getting to know God—remembering who he is, rehearsing who he is, and deepening our understanding of who he is. So, bathe your mind in Scripture (Romans 12:2; 2 Timothy 3:16–17). Build habits into your life that include personal time with the Lord as well as consistent time with his people. Those people are very helpful in reminding you about who God is.

It's also important to give yourself tangible reminders of God's faithfulness and his attributes. Maybe it's journal entries, a piece of artwork, a special mug, a piece of jewelry, or regular meetings with friends where you talk about God's work in your life in the interim. Intentional habits and even physical mementos that direct your attention to who God is and spark your memory of who you know him to be are invaluable in times of waiting. Also, know that as our histories with God build, so too does our trust in him. Maybe you don't have a long history with God just yet. That's okay! Just like any relationship, your relationship with God will have times of incredible growth and exhilaration, times of seeming dryness, and times of mundanity. Your relationship with him lasts a lifetime, so allow it time and space to build. He remains faithful in every season; we just need to keep pressing in.

REHEARSING GOD'S HISTORY—PSALM 27:2-3

After declaring who God has been in his life and having no need for fear, David boldly states that when people come against him, it is they who are defeated. David could be referring to specific past events, such as his defeat of Goliath (1 Samuel 17). He also seems to be confident God will defeat his enemies this time.

Recalling God's past faithfulness to us and others is powerful. The Bible is filled with accounts of the ways God works on behalf of his people; so is Christian history. One-for-one mapping of Bible stories onto our lives is not a sound method of exegesis. However, God does not change, and the accounts in the Bible are written for our instruction (1 Corinthians 10:6; Hebrews 12:1–2). So, we should receive his encouragement from the ways he has worked with his people in the past. And, as we do with so many others, it is reasonable to learn by example and through story. Hebrews 11 is a great summary of some specific accounts.

The exodus is a persistent theme throughout the Bible that often reminds me of the grander redemptive arc and God's faithfulness throughout each stage. I sometimes consider how the Israelites wanted to return to Egypt, but God had much better things in store. When I feel overwhelmed in the waiting and am tempted to return to old things, I think of how silly it seemed for Israel to desire slavery instead of freedom. When a solution to something seems impossible, I think of Abraham and Sarah who conceived Isaac despite her being "past the age" and "him as good as dead" (Hebrews 11:11–12). When I feel discouraged and wonder if God is paying attention, I think of Hagar who called God "a God of seeing" (Genesis 16:13). I think of the reality that God "heard [the] groaning" of the Israelites who were enslaved in Egypt, "remembered his covenant with Abraham," "saw the people of Israel—and God knew" (Exodus 2:24–25). God sees, hears, and acts. I know this from the Bible.

I also know it from my own life; God has proven faithful time and time again. I remind myself of the ways he worked through a knee injury and all the good that has ultimately come from it. I think of the healing and freedom he has brought to past hurts, recalling how challenging those seasons were but also seeing how God uprooted lies so life could come forth. I consider the people who have come alongside my family. I think of visual depictions God has impressed on me that relate to a truth about who he is. This history gives me specific touchpoints to know God will come through again. I may not know how or when, but I can declare that he is good, and his purposes prevail.

If you've never intentionally considered your history with God, I would highly recommend it. There are myriad ways to do this: write it out, depict it artistically, put a tangible reminder in your home, and share it with others. The "call to remember" is throughout God's Word. Think of all the tangible ways he has given his people to do this—the Passover (Exodus 12), the stones from the Jordan (Joshua 4), and communion (1 Corinthians 11:23–26). We naturally forget, and we are easily distracted by the world and deceived by our sinfulness as well as by Satan, so we need to take steps to intentionally remember who God is and what he has done.

When you have new experiences of God's faithfulness, add them to your "memory bank," as my aunt would say. Someone I knew kept a spreadsheet with important happenings in her life; I liked the idea, so I have a document that lists general dates and major events. Often counselors will ask clients to chart their life histories to see themes. We can keep these running histories to help us pay attention to what God is doing. And we can revisit them to remind us of his faithfulness.

You might be surprised at how God uses these intentional memorials. You might be surprised by how he uses unintentional ones too! Thanks to an impactful sermon series from a prior pastor, I've long loved John 10:10 and John 15. When I moved into my home, my sister helped me decorate. I'm a words girl and a bit of a minimalist, thus much of my décor is simply signs. In my living room hang two signs my sister made. One says, "Abide in Me," and the other says, "Abundant Life." In telling a friend about how the word *abide* was an important word for me in 2024, she said, "Oh, like the sign in your house." I'd completely forgotten! In my pondering over God sparking a dream to write a book, and my newfound sense of wonder in the possibilities of the future, I noticed two signs above my trash can. One says, "Imagine life's possibilities," and the other, "Believe in your dreams." Abide, imagine, dream—all wrapped up in abundant life. Yes, this is what God was stirring in my heart. And he used signs that had been in my house for seven years, that had essentially become background noise, to confirm it. The sign over my couch? "Be still and know." Ah, yes—wait, abide, be still, know that there is abundant life in Christ, and dare to dream. How faithful of God to remind me of these truths and invite me into a new adventure of trust. This is a story I'll be adding to my history to pull out whenever I need a reminder that God really does see and that I really can be confident in him.

Let me add that it's fun to cultivate a mindset that expects God to be at work in our daily lives—a mindset of anticipation. Obviously, anything we think we see God doing or we think we sense the Holy Spirit impressing on us needs to line up with what we know to be true of God, which comes from knowing his Word. But recalling that we have a personal relationship with the Creator of the universe, that the Holy Spirit indwells us when we put our faith in Jesus (Ephesians 1:3–14), and that God often works through ordinary means, it shouldn't surprise us to see consistent evidence of his care and faithfulness. As with most things, the more we look for it, the more we see.

Let's start with the obvious ways we see God in our lives on a daily basis. Friends, family, physical health, financial provision, good food, opportunities for refreshment, laughter, interesting stories, and the like are all things for which we should be thanking and praising God. James 1:17 says, "Every good gift and every perfect gift is from above, coming down from the Father of lights, with whom there is no variation or shadow due to change." Colossians 3:17 encourages, "And whatever you do, in word or deed, do everything in the name of the Lord Jesus, giving thanks to God the Father through him." Simply thanking God for the things we often take for granted can help attune our eyes and hearts to the things he does.

We also notice God in the beauty of creation around us. Living in Colorado, I have ample opportunity to see the grandeur and majesty of God in creation. When I look at the mountains, I often intentionally pause to thank God for the reminder of his power and vastness. The mountains make me feel secure. In part, this is because I'm directionally challenged, so knowing which way is west and which mountain my house is close to gives me confidence I can always make it home. In seriousness, though, something as simple as your daily view of creation can be a persistent reminder of the deep truths of God. For me, that's safety and mountains. For you, maybe it's the ocean and vastness, or the forest and protection, or flowers and beauty, or something completely different. There are thousands, even millions, of ways God's character is demonstrated through creation.

Perhaps my favorite way of seeing God's faithfulness in the daily things of life is through what my mom refers to as "love notes from God." These are the tiniest of things that come at just the right time in just the right way to remind you that you are seen, known, and loved by your Creator. For me, it's often an encouraging email in the middle of a hard work week or someone saying hello or smiling at the gym on a day I was feeling unseen. Sometimes it's a canceled social plan when I'm feeling overwhelmed. Other times it's a funny thought or comment or song that breaks through a mental spiral. Sometimes it's getting to help another person, to be the one who smiles and sees how meaningful it is, or to have someone share deeply with me unprompted. Often, these things aren't even when I'm feeling down; they're just things filling the encouragement tank, letting me know there is a lot of goodness in our lives, serving as touchpoints to go back to later.

Notice these things, praise God for them, and tell others what happened. Again, the more we open our eyes, the more we see God at work. And the more we see God, the more we trust him. Be grateful and express it regularly—to God and others. First Thessalonians 5:16–18 says, "Rejoice always, pray without ceasing, give thanks in all circumstances; for this is the will of God in Christ Jesus for you."

CHAPTER 4

YEARNING FOR THE FUTURE

Yearning for the future is perhaps the most prominent perspective in our waiting. It's often easy to envision a better future and want to be there—now! This is not quite the type of yearning for the future I have in mind when talking about waiting and abiding. Again, waiting is not all about the circumstances; it's an invitation to abide. If we set our eyes and hearts solely on a circumstantial change, we're bound to be disappointed and make ourselves pretty miserable in the meantime. Even so, waiting and abiding are not about denying our longings or ridding ourselves of desire. There is, indeed, a better future; we should yearn for it! So, what does this look like? David's psalm gives us some help.

ETERNAL PERSPECTIVE—PSALM 27:4

Psalm 27:4 is likely familiar to you: "One thing have I asked of the LORD, that will I seek after: that I may dwell in the house of the LORD all the days of my life, to gaze upon the beauty of the LORD and to inquire in his temple." This is a central theme—David simply wants to be with the Lord. He is referring to the physical tabernacle here. So, David would need physical rescue from his enemies to get there. But notice how his focus is on dwelling (abiding) with God. He wants to look upon God's beauty. He wants to "inquire" or "meditate" or "seek." Essentially, David wants to be with God and know him intimately.

This is crucial in our waiting. Yes, we pray for whatever circumstance our waiting is about. God really does care about our earthly lives and daily experiences—they matter in a very real way. But ultimately, our deepest longings will only be filled by God. We are humans who were designed for a relationship with our Creator and with one another, but we currently live in a world that does not allow for the fullness of that design to be expressed. Our central longing, the one that undergirds every other longing, is for final restoration. Our truest and deepest desire is for all to be made right. That yearning is something only God is big enough to hold, and only he can sustain us through it. So, we seek God's presence first, not his provision. Or, to put it another way, we seek his face before seeking his hand. While we do want his provision for any given circumstance, what we most need is for God to be with us. And what we ultimately long for is to be with God (John 14:1–3; 17:24; Revelation 21:3–4).

My dad is a great illustration of what it means to seek someone's presence more than their provision. Whenever I would visit him—when he was living at home and later at the nursing home—his face would light up. I knew I was deeply loved, and he simply enjoyed my presence. Yet, I would often offer, or he would request, some type of practical help. Despite that practical help, what he most desired was to spend time with me. My dad ultimately wasn't interested in what I could do for him; he just wanted to spend time with me. He desired my presence, and my provision was merely a bonus. The reality that satisfied him most was that I came, not what I did while I was there.

Similarly, when we seek God for who he is, not primarily for what he can do, we experience the satisfaction of his presence. Because God is who he is, he provides for our practical needs as well. It brings him honor when we present our requests to him (Philippians 4:6). But we present our requests primarily because we know who he is and trust him. So, even in seeking God's provision, we first and foremost seek God himself. And it is in him that we find the deepest satisfaction.

PRESENT REALITY—A FORETASTE OF THE ETERNAL

Though the fullness of our being with God is something yet future, God's presence is something we experience even now. The concept of God with us struck me in a new way during my season of intense waiting. I often thought of God going before me and preparing the way, directing my steps, or even being "next to" or "beside" me. But I recognized that sometimes my mindset was more of God giving wisdom or clearing a path, and less of him being with me in all of it. God does, indeed, direct our steps and prepare the way. We do need his wisdom, and we do need to walk in obedience. But God does not merely give us directives to accomplish on our own. Nor is he an outside observer to whom we report in prayer or someone far off sending communiques. He's not even just next to us as an outside observer. He is intimately present with us in everything.

We know Jesus is Immanuel, God with us (Matthew 1:22–23). What does it mean that he is with us? Jesus has fully experienced human life. Hebrews 2:14–17 explains, "Since therefore the children share in flesh and blood, he himself likewise partook of the same things … he helps the offspring of Abraham. Therefore he had to be made like his brothers in every respect, so that he might become a merciful and faithful high priest in the service of God" (see also Hebrews 4:14–16).

In short, Jesus gets it! God is not just our Creator; God the Son has experienced a real human life. He lived a normal life with actual people. Our risen Savior in heaven knows what our lives are like, and he "lives to make intercession" for us (Hebrews 7:25). When Jesus gave the Great Commission, he included the promise that "I am with you always, to the end of the age" (Matthew 28:20). He told his followers to, "Go therefore and make disciples of all nations, baptizing them in the name of the Father and of the Son and of the Holy Spirit, teaching them to observe all that I have commanded you" (Matthew 28:18–20) but not on their own. He would be with them always, to the very end. He is with us still today!

If you are in Christ, the Holy Spirit resides in you (Romans 8:9–17; Ephesians 1:11–14; Philippians 2:12–13). That means everywhere you are, God is with you. We do not have to go to a tabernacle or temple to know the presence of God (John 4:23–24; 14:16–17). The temple veil tore when Jesus was crucified (Matthew 27:51). "We have confidence to enter the holy places by the blood of Jesus" (Hebrews 10:19). We "have received the Spirit of adoption as sons, by whom we cry, 'Abba! Father!'" (Romans 8:15). "The Spirit helps us in our weakness. For we do not know what to pray for as we ought, but the Spirit himself intercedes for us with groanings too deep for words. And he who searches hearts knows what is the mind of the Spirit, because the Spirit intercedes for the saints according to the will of God" (Romans 8:26–27). It is not just that God is with us in the sense of his omnipresence or because Jesus lived a real human life. The Holy Spirit—one of the three persons of the Trinity—actually indwells you. Not only is there no place you can go that he is not (Psalm 139:7–12), but he is in you.

Yet God being with us includes more than the reality of Jesus' promise and the indwelling Holy Spirit. It is not just that God is with us; we are invited into the presence of God—to abide with him. We must spend time with him intentionally through things like studying the Bible so as to know how he reveals himself, praying to commune with him, and participating in his family through corporate worship and fellowship. Even Jesus—God in human flesh—"would withdraw to desolate places and pray" (Luke 5:16). Spending intentional time with God, both alone and corporately, matters greatly. Even so, being in God's presence does not always have to be formal. God is present everywhere in the world. We can be in God's presence when we pray throughout the day, when we recognize his beauty and give him praise for it, when we are pained and cry over the realities of brokenness, when we seek wisdom, when we yearn for wholeness, and when we love others with his love. All of life is lived with and unto the Lord.

God's presence and our circumstances are not separate things but are intricately intertwined. While our deepest longings are for eternity, we do not have to wait until then to experience foretastes. In a funny way, it can be compared to baking brownies—we get to lick the batter bowl and enjoy the aroma of chocolate wafting from the oven while waiting for the brownies to fully bake. And some of us enjoy taking that first little bite fresh out of the oven, "just to make sure they'll be okay for the guests," before savoring a full serving when they arrive. We genuinely experience God's presence here, even if not in its fullness. God really is in our day-to-day world, and we really can be with him in our day-to-day lives. Physical realities, human relationships, and earth-bound accomplishments matter. After all, the creation of this world was God's idea, and he declared it good (Genesis 1).

Moses' prayer in Psalm 90 highlights the perspective that eternity gives on the temporal. He lauded God's eternality by praying, "Before the mountains were brought forth, or ever you had formed the earth and the world, from everlasting to everlasting you are God" (v. 2). In contrast, "the years of our life are seventy, or even by reason of strength eighty" (v. 10) and we return to dust (v. 3). In light of these truths, Moses prayed, "So teach us to number our days that we may get a heart of wisdom ... Let the favor of the Lord our God be upon us, and establish the work of our hands upon us; yes, establish the work of our hands!" (vv. 12, 17). God is eternal; we are not; thus, we need to be wise with our days (Ephesians 5:15–17). Our days and our time on this earth matter—to the people whose lives we touch and to God's eternal purposes. They also matter in how we get to know, love, and worship God. He created time, and we experience him in the context of the time he has entrusted to us. The accounts of the Bible show us how God works through everyday situations in the lives of real people. He does the same in our lives. So, we are right to care about our temporal realities.

God also created us to live with him for eternity (2 Peter 3:9–13). When we begin to see ourselves within the bigger story, it both increases our understanding of the importance of our lives and releases our grip on them. When we focus on the bigger picture—longing for God's presence and the completion of his ultimate purposes—it becomes easier to trust and see that God is writing our story in the best way. We can experience the foretastes in all their deliciousness while knowing the completed creation will be far beyond what we can imagine.

When we recognize that God cares about our circumstances and our deepest longing is for him, we have the right perspective. The things for which we are waiting matter, but they are not what matters most. The more time we spend in God's presence, the more we trust him, and thus, the more we trust his plan. Our hearts begin to orient toward him above our circumstances, and, consequently, we can wait effectively.

EXPECTANT AND HUMBLE—PSALM 27:5–10

After naming his foremost desire, David turns back to extolling God and conveying confidence that God will deliver him. He believes God will protect him in times of turmoil: "He will hide me in his shelter in the day of trouble; he will conceal me under the cover of his tent; he will lift me high upon a rock" (Psalm 27:5). David believes God will give the victory in his current distress, and when he does, he will praise. He will "offer in his tent sacrifices with shouts of joy; I will sing and make melody to the LORD" (Psalm 27:6). So confident is David that he is already envisioning being at the tabernacle praising God.

But despite his confidence, David still experiences fear. He calls on God to hear him and be gracious. He pleads with God to not forsake him like others have (Psalm 27:7–10). Notice that David does not plead with God on the merits of his own righteousness or by offering anything to God. He simply acknowledges his desperation and desire. This is our condition in Christ too. We do not earn salvation on our own merit (Ephesians 2:1–10; Titus 3:5), nor can we manipulate God to answer our prayers based on anything we do or bring. Instead, we rely solely on him and his righteousness (John 15:7, 16; Hebrews 4:14–16; 10:19–23; 1 John 3:19–24; 5:13–15).

I wonder if this tension between confidence and fear resonates with you. Do you ever find it difficult to honestly yearn for a specific earthly future? Do you ever find yourself knowing you can be confident in God, and yet fearful about how things will actually turn out? Have you ever tried to minimize your desires in an attempt to shield yourself from disappointment? I know I have. It's scary to be real about the things we want in this life, knowing they may not come to fruition. It's hard to cling to the truth of who God is even when we know we won't always understand what he does. But we can neither minimize who God is nor ignore the things that are in our hearts. If we do, we're not being honest. And if we don't bring our full hearts before the Lord, we won't experience the full benefits of his presence. We might miss out on his provision for us too.

My recent experience has been instructive to me. As mentioned in the introduction, a time of organizational growing pain at my place of employment coincided with God reigniting my passion for leadership. The organization was at a point in its history where a shift in structure, strategy, and culture was needed for continued thriving. The opportunities for greater team collaboration and increased effectiveness were enormous. God had used my personal burnout to bring some of these organizational blind spots and opportunities to light, so I was particularly invested in helping the organization grow. I stepped into an informal leadership role and became an agent of change. I envisioned various related futures for the organization and for my role, and I allowed myself to genuinely long for them.

But change is not easy. While some shared my vision and passion, not everyone did. There was resistance and confusion about the path forward. Miscommunications, misunderstandings, and unique relational dynamics added to the challenge. My excitement was tempered by exhaustion and disappointment. At one point in the process, God called me to step aside from being an agent and promoter of change—to let go of my vision and leave change in the hands of others while I continued in my normal role. God equipped me daily to navigate the situation. His presence was evident, and my confidence in who he is was emboldened. But my uncertainty and fear about the future were also real.

I love that, even in his fear, David declares, "But the LORD will take me in" (Psalm 27:10). This conveys a deep trust in the character of God. It also demonstrates humility. I found God to be trustworthy in my circumstances. Every time I feared and yet stood firm in him, he gave me the strength and encouragement I needed. I also began to see how the work God was doing in my life was contributing to his work in the lives of others. My stepping away from promoting change and continuing only in my regular position provided space for others to experience personal growth and to have more ownership in the organizational transition. It also provided space for God to do necessary refining work in me, open my eyes to opportunities outside of work, and deepen my understanding of abiding. My recognition of my need for him grew, and I discovered more aspects of his character. The depth of my disappointment was related to the depth of my longing, and the depth of both was related to the depth at which God sanctified me and grew my trust in him. Had I not allowed myself to be honest, I would have missed the richness of God's presence, and thus, deeper satisfaction in him.

God used my honesty about the initial organizational dream to direct me to a deeper dream related to the way he designed me. The spark of passion for my workplace wasn't just about structure and collaboration at work, it was a yearning for people to know and fully live out their design as God intended. It was a desire for people to deeply know God, know how he created them, and steward those gifts and opportunities for his glory. Were I not real about my longings for specific change at the organization, I would have missed the opportunity to be redirected. I also needed to experience both the longing and the disappointment to see that the actual desire God placed in my heart was something greater, and its outworking happened in a variety of venues. I needed him to show me that, ultimately, I serve him, and the gifts and passions he's given me are intended to be used everywhere I am, not just at my job. I needed to explore the depth of my passion to allow God to clarify it. I needed to give energy to my heart's yearning so God could cultivate it and direct it. Trying to pretend I didn't want what I did would have been dishonest—with myself and before the Lord. Ignoring my fears would have denied God's quelling of them. Keeping God out of my longing—and disappointment—would have prevented me from being able to experience him. And that would have been the worst loss of all.

He also used the season to give me a brand-new dream. When God called me to step back from leading organizational change, he also planted the desire to write this book! All that passion had a new outpouring. Writing this has helped me process the lessons God was teaching me in that season. It has also solidified my love for discipleship and for people to know God, love him, and live according to their unique design. I hope the account of what God has done in my life is giving you a helpful visual to latch onto these truths about abiding and waiting.

Interestingly, my honesty about my circumstantial longings led me to a deeper hunger for and experience of God's presence in the larger eternal sense too. By allowing my hunger for things on this earth to grow, my hunger for God and final redemption grows all the more. God satisfied my longings, not through the earthly change I initially desired but in my relationship with him. Though I admittedly still waver, wrestle, and wonder about various life situations, I'm finding that the richness of God's presence allows me to trust him with circumstances and let go of my desired outcomes. I am more able to genuinely say, "Nevertheless, not my will, but yours, be done" (Luke 22:42). I am more in awe of who God is and more enraptured by his grander story. In seeking God's face, I find that I can trust his hand.

I don't know what you are waiting for or what fears are in the mix. But I do know that, in our waiting, we can boldly declare who God is and be honest about our fears. We know that in Christ our eternity is completely secure (John 10:28–30; Jude 1:24–25). We also know God sees us and cares for us; he will not forsake us (Hebrews 13:5–6). So, we can cry out to God in our need, admit our fears, and remind our hearts to trust in him, knowing he hears us and cares for us (Matthew 6:25–34; Philippians 4:4–8; 1 Peter 5:6–7). We can come before him, fully present, to seek his presence. The more of our hearts we bare before him, the more of his fullness we experience.

SEEKING GOD'S FACE

Like David, in our confidence and fear, and even in our mundane, we are to seek God's face (Psalm 27:8). To seek God's face is to pursue his presence and favor. Notice how this is oriented both toward the future and the present. David seeks God's face now, with future longing. It is God who has instructed David to seek his face; God desires a relationship, and David actively engages. God is real and personal, and a relationship with him is a two-way street. He sought us first (Genesis 3:15; Romans 5:8; Ephesians 2:1–10). "We love because he first loved us" (1 John 4:19). Our eternal righteousness depends entirely on him (2 Corinthians 5:17–21). But his love calls for a response.

We continue to seek God's face because he sought us, and true life is in him. Consider passages like Philippians 2:12–13, which says, "Work out your own salvation with fear and trembling, for it is God who works in you, both to will and to work for his good pleasure." God is the one at work, and we actively participate. Similarly, Romans 12:1–2 says, "I appeal to you therefore, brothers, by the mercies of God, to present your bodies as a living sacrifice, holy and acceptable to God, which is your spiritual worship. Do not be conformed to this world, but be transformed by the renewal of your mind, that by testing you may discern what is the will of God, what is good and acceptable and perfect." We seek God's face by actively engaging with him, living all of our lives as a response to who he is and what he does. We intentionally seek renewal of our minds, wanting them to be conformed to truth so that we can know God.

Second Peter 1:3 says, in part, "His divine power has granted to us all things that pertain to life and godliness." Verses 5–7 continue, "For this very reason, make every effort to supplement your faith with virtue, and virtue with knowledge, and knowledge with self-control, and self-control with steadfastness, and steadfastness with godliness, and godliness with brotherly affection, and brotherly affection with love." We see, again, that God is the one who equips and accomplishes the work of sanctification (Philippians 1:6), and yet we are also to participate. We seek God's face when we set sin aside and instead actively live the way God calls us to.

Seeking God is not only about our private times with him or personal purity; it's also about other people. Notice how Peter mentions "godliness with brotherly affection, and brotherly affection with love" (2 Peter 1:7). John writes, "This commandment we have from him: whoever loves God must also love his brother" (1 John 4:21). The New Testament "one anothers" speak to the reality of living out God's call within community. Most of the epistles were written to churches, not individuals; the "you" is often plural—"all y'all." We seek God's face together, and we experience God's face as we love one another with the love of Christ.

Hebrews 10:19–25 combines these concepts nicely. It speaks of our confidence to enter into God's presence through the blood of Jesus, our ability to draw near to him with assurance, the reality that God is faithful so we can stand firm, and the way we need community to stir us up "to love and good works … encouraging one another." We can seek God's face with confidence because of what he has accomplished. We do it personally, we do it privately, we do it in community, and we do it publicly. In all the ways we experience life, we can seek God's face.

Returning to David, he knew God invited him to seek the

presence and favor of the Lord, so David did. We, too, are invited to seek the presence and favor of the Lord because he has sought us. Just like David, we need never fear that God will forsake us (1 John 3:1–3). So, we can seek him with confidence, humility, and intentionality. As we do, he will sustain us. He will be with us in our waiting, sustaining us as we abide in him.

CHAPTER 5

LIVING IN THE PRESENT—
OBEDIENCE

After we've remembered and looked ahead, we are left with where we are: waiting in the present. But before we talk about living in the present, did you notice how remembering the past and yearning for the future are present actions? The past, present, and future are not as disconnected as we sometimes think. God gave us the full redemptive narrative for a reason. Knowing the beginning and the end enables us to effectively live in the middle. We need to actually *live* in the middle. Waiting is not idle, and what happens in the waiting matters.

Perhaps most obvious and yet most easy to overlook, this entire psalm is a prayer. Prayer is crucial to living in the present! Because prayer is such a big topic, we'll discuss prayer in a later chapter. I just didn't want you to miss it as the first, best, practical step.

In the preceding chapter, I talked about seeking God's face as part of yearning for the future and living in the present. God's presence is a "both/and" reality. It is both something we currently experience and something we look forward to in the future. We seek God's face in our yearning, coming to him in honesty, casting our fears on him, and standing firm in him with trust. This happens through things like prayer, studying God's Word to get to know him, actively obeying God, and spending time with other believers. As we do those things, we are both seeking his face within the context of eternal promise and the context of our day-to-day lives. God's presence is something we experience in the present. Just as he invited David to seek his face, we, too, are invited into the same (John 17:20–26; Hebrews 4:14–16; 10:19–25).

As David's psalm progresses, he describes some practical ways to seek God's presence. In the previous chapter, I discussed how responding to God in obedience is one way we seek his face. David affirms this in Psalm 27:11.

OBEDIENCE—PSALM 27:11

David is praying. He has declared his trust in the Lord, recalled God's faithfulness, expressed yearning for a different future, and set himself to seek God's face. What does he do next? David intentionally directs his heart toward obedience to God. He says, "Teach me your way, O LORD, and lead me on a level path because of my enemies." He wants to live as God would have him live. God is the giver of life, and thus his ways are life. The only way to be on a "level path" is to walk with God.

Passages like 1 Peter 1 give us a right perspective on obedience. Only after describing the stunning reality and permanence of salvation does Peter call believers to walk in holiness. He talks of being "born again to a living hope through the resurrection of Jesus Christ from the dead, to an inheritance that is imperishable, undefiled, and unfading, kept in heaven for you" (vv. 3–4). He talks of rejoicing and steadfastness during trial "so that the tested genuineness of your faith—more precious than gold that perishes though it is tested by fire—may be found to result in praise and glory and honor at the revelation of Jesus Christ" (v. 7). He speaks of the prophets having prophesied about and inquired into salvation: "They were serving not themselves but you, in the things that have now been announced to you through those who preached the good news to you by the Holy Spirit sent from heaven, things into which angels long to look" (v. 12). Salvation is quite stunning!

Peter continues, "Therefore, preparing your minds for action, and being sober-minded, set your hope fully on the grace that will be brought to you at the revelation of Jesus Christ. As obedient children, do not be conformed to the passions of your former ignorance, but as he who called you is holy, you also be holy in all your conduct" (vv. 13–15). Obedience does not garner salvation. Rather, it is only because we are saved that we seek to live a holy life. Jesus told his followers, "If you keep my commandments, you will abide in my love, just as I have kept my Father's commandments and abide in his love. These things I have spoken to you, that my joy may be in you, and that your joy may be full" (John 15:10–11). We do not obey to earn God's love. Rather, because we are loved, we obey (1 John 4:13–20). Because we trust God, we follow him (James 2:14–26; 1 John 1:6—2:6).

Interestingly, David links his request with the reality of his enemies. When experiencing hardship or uncertainty or extended periods of waiting, it can be especially difficult to obey God. And it can be especially difficult to hear his voice or discern his will. No one said following God is easy! But we are certainly not on our own. Philippians 2:12–13 calls us to "work out your own salvation with fear and trembling, for it is God who works in you, both to will and to work for his good pleasure." Philippians 1:6 encourages us that God will complete his good work in us. We actively submit to God, desiring to honor him because he is worthy and his ways are best, but also knowing our holiness ultimately does not depend on us—it depends on him. On this side of the cross, believers have the advantage of the indwelling Holy Spirit. We are never alone because he is always with us. God is actively at work in transforming us, and he can equip us and carry us through any obedience challenge we might face (Romans 8:26–30; 1 Corinthians 10:13; Jude 1:24–25).

We also have the truth of God's written Word. The Bible is filled with instructions about God's way. We don't need any special insight to know that we are called to love others, speak truth, forgive, flee sexual immorality, remain in Christian community, or the like. One way we wait on the Lord and experience his presence is simply through obeying him in what he has already revealed to us. If you're looking for some quick reminders, I always enjoy Romans 12, Galatians 5, Ephesians 4, and Colossians 3. You might also check out Hebrews 10 and 12. And remember, these aren't things you are to do through self-effort; they are enabled by the Holy Spirit and done with the support of the Christian community.

Obedience is not easy, and it does not guarantee pleasant-in-the-moment circumstances or even necessarily make our waiting any easier. Consider David's situation in this psalm; as far as we know, he was not being pursued by enemies because of any sin of his own. Yet, he still seeks to obey God and knows that only God's ways will lead to a level path. Or think about Joseph of the Old Testament who was sold by his brothers and imprisoned yet remained faithful throughout (Genesis 37—50). Or consider Joseph of the New Testament who was likely shamed for seeming to have had an illegitimate child (Matthew 1—2). Jesus' own parents were not immune to hardship. Consider the faithful listed in Hebrews 11, those who "did not receive what was promised, since God had provided something better for us, that apart from us they should not be made perfect" (vv. 39–40). Obedience does not always mean we receive our desired outcome and certainly not in our desired timeline. But God is worthy of our obedience simply because of who he is. Also, as our Creator, God knows what is best. Disobedience will never lead to good ends; obedience is always the better option.

Obedience is not just about setting ourselves up for better circumstances; it is a key part of seeking God's face. Living God's way is part of deepening our relationship with him, much like happens with friends. We don't typically obey our friends, but we're often willing to do things our friends enjoy simply to be with them and give them pleasure. When we do, we often end up getting to know them in different ways, making our relationship closer. Many times, we end up becoming more like one another too. Have you ever found a new favorite treat because your friend introduced you to it? Or taken up a new hobby just to spend time with your friend only to later discover that you enjoy the activity itself? The people we spend time with tend to rub off on us. This is part of why it matters with whom we choose to be in close relationship (1 Corinthians 15:33; 2 Corinthians 6:14–18). This same deepening of connection and "rubbing off" happens with God. The more we follow God's direction and do so in ways that reflect him, the better we know God, the more we rest in him, and the more we are like him. In short, obedience is a major part of abiding in God. And the abiding life is the abundant life!

Easy to say and hard to live, right? Of course, we recognize that obedience will be hard because it often requires denying our sinful desires or doing things differently than the surrounding culture. God's ways aren't natural to us. Plus, they often take time. And when we're waiting, we're not always in the mood to slow down! But I don't think those are the only challenges. What do you do when you know God has asked you to do something but people around you are unsupportive or simply don't understand why? What if your obedience causes pain for someone else? Or what if you step into God's call, but then the old thing beckons you back?

What if that old thing beckons you back with a promise to be new, better, or different somehow? What if the new thing has challenges you didn't expect? When you hear God clearly and the landscape seems to change, do you remain faithful to God's call, or do you waver?

My intense season of waiting involved many of these challenges. As explained in Chapter 4, I had been an initiator and champion of needed organizational reflection and change at my place of work. The possibilities—for the organization, my coworkers, and myself—invigorated me. I was hopeful about the future and eager to be a part of forward progress. I had a clear dream for which I was patiently waiting. But barriers persisted, other relevant factors came to light, and it became evident that God was calling me to step aside from informal leadership and remain active only in my official role. The decision was made through an unfolding process with confirmation from a variety of sources, so there was no denying the step of obedience God was asking me to take. But it was messy! As I was preparing to announce my decision, the organization appeared to take tangible steps toward the future I'd envisioned. I wavered. Did I really have to step aside? Thankfully, God provided family members to remind me to stand firm. I also wrote down all the ways God had made the call evident to reaffirm it to myself. And, of course, I prayed! In his grace, God made the process simple for me. He also bore positive fruit from my obedience—both for me and the organization—nearly immediately. Obviously, that doesn't happen every time, but it certainly helped me stand firm. I had heard and heeded the call, and what a relief it was.

Even so, not all the fruit felt positive. Relationships were harmed. Not everyone in the organization understood my choice, feeling like I'd let them down. I felt like I had to defend my choice, which I did not always do with an attitude of love. Sin reared its head in my heart as I struggled with a critical spirit. That was a lesson in how to stand firm in God's call no matter the narrative or reaction from others. It was also a lesson in learning to walk in God's ways even when it is painful. I wanted to complain or blame or be defensive or throw myself a pity party. At times, I wanted to withhold positive contributions I could still make in my current capacity. But God called me to simply obey and trust, to stand firm, to give selflessly, and to do it for his glory with an attitude reflective of his love. I had been asked to obey in something big. Now, I was being asked to obey in the daily portion. It is not just what we do that matters; how we go about it is often the larger obedience challenge. I needed humility, courage, and steadfastness. Would I stand with integrity? Would I serve sacrificially to the glory of God? Or would I adopt a victim mentality or resort to people-pleasing instead? Wrestling with these issues in my own heart was the first order of business. Then relational repair began.

To my surprise, I had to reaffirm the choice to myself continually. It was an intentional adjustment to live in a new season despite the relief and freedom with which it came. Not only had God called me out of the concerted change effort at my job, but he had called me into brand new things outside of work. Those were exhilarating! And, yet, I still wanted the prior dream. In some ways, I was being asked to walk but found myself wanting to wait instead. One time in particular it seemed like I could return to a leadership role in organizational change, only with a promise that it would be better this time. Certainly, God can do that. His character is unchanging, and his call for us to love others and live in truth is consistent, but the specific outworking looks different in different seasons. Oh, how I wanted that to be the case! But, again, outside voices—family, friends, and even a church sermon—confirmed it was not the time. In my heart of hearts, I knew. This was a call to remain steadfast. And, in his graciousness, God gave me just what I needed to stand firm before removing the apparent opportunity, and thus the temptation.

I don't know what your obedience challenge is. But I know, for all of us, the impulse to "return to Egypt" is strong. The familiar is comfortable. Perhaps more enticing is the fruit that looks good for food, delights the eyes, and seems to give wisdom (Genesis 3:6). Promise is alluring. For me, it felt like I'd been invited to go into a Canaan of sorts—into a new thing where my identity wasn't linked to my job and where my giftings were to be used in unexpected ways and new avenues. But when I spied it out, I saw both the fertile, fruitful land that I so wanted and some pretty scary giants (Numbers 13—14). Would I be like Caleb and Joshua, knowing that the God who rescued the Israelites from Egypt would certainly clear the land of the giants? Or would I be like the rest of the Israelites and try to return to some vision of a past that never existed in the first place (see Exodus 16:3 and compare it to Exodus 1)? Would I follow God's call with boldness and trust, or would I turn back in fear? After so much waiting, some of us aren't sure we want to go into the new thing.

Temptations are very real! They come in all shapes and sizes, and they're everywhere we look. But temptation is an invitation into deeper maturity and closer abiding. Temptations challenge us to not be deceived but to affirm that "every good gift and every perfect gift is from above, coming down from the Father of lights, with whom there is no variation or shadow due to change. Of his own will he brought us forth by the word of truth, that we should be a kind of first-fruits of his creatures" (James 1:17–18). We can be encouraged that "no temptation has overtaken you that is not common to man. God is faithful, and he will not let you be tempted beyond your ability, but with the temptation he will also provide the way of escape, that you may be able to endure it" (1 Corinthians 10:13).

For me, the challenge was to wait and walk simultaneously. I had both a new dream with open avenues and a dream that had been awakened but seemed to be in wait mode. Would I hold onto both? Would I give myself fully to the new while also still actively waiting? Would I lay my desires before God, even to the point of allowing a dream to die if it was a false one? Would I walk forward, with confidence and trust, in the ways he called me? Would I stand steadfast in the areas where he was calling me to remain? Perhaps the bigger challenge, would I do it all with a heart inclined to him, seeking his glory, and seeking to let him transform my character? Would I be more concerned with the circumstances or with my relationship with God? God was asking me to rely on him, trust him, submit to him, and live fully present. He was asking me to both wait and walk and to do so in a way that honors and reflects him. My guess is that your life is characterized by similar circumstances. Rarely are we only ever doing one thing. So, I'm fairly confident he's asking you to wait and walk and trust and be transformed. He's asking you to abide.

Obedience is seldom a one-time choice, and intense periods of waiting make it even harder. But it matters—in small things and big things. Thus, we need to abide continually. God will equip us (2 Peter 1:3). He will provide us with what we need—the confirmation of his Word, the power of the indwelling Holy Spirit, the encouragement of community, and the courage we did not know we would need. Keep trusting and leaning in.

Remain in the Word in every season, have wise counselors who love you and love God, pray, and invite others to pray with you and for you. Rely on the Holy Spirit. You have stories of God's faithfulness in the past. You have stories of your faithfulness to him. You know he is training you, and that training is good (Hebrews 12:1–13). So, be encouraged! The habits you are learning now are the habits that will carry into your next season. It is through being faithful in each thing that is before us currently, no matter how small or large, that we learn to remain faithful to the end. Obedience requires courage and perseverance, and it is always worth it! God will be faithful to the end (Jude 1:24–25), so we can obey without fear (1 John 4:17–21). The real habit we're developing is lifelong abiding in Christ. And, oh, what a glorious day it will be when that habit is reality in its fullness!

CHAPTER 6

LIVING IN THE PRESENT— ENEMIES AND COURAGE

The Christian life is not unopposed. Have you ever heard that? It's true. Not only do we have our own sin to contend with, other people make things difficult for us, and we have a spiritual enemy. We need to be aware of all of this if we are going to abide in the present effectively.

We've already talked about obedience, something David asked God to help him with, which he also linked to enemies. But David also asks God for specific protection against enemies. David writes, "Give me not up to the will of my adversaries; for false witnesses have risen against me, and they breathe out violence" (Psalm 27:12). Obedience doesn't mean enemies go away or bad things don't happen. Abiding does not mean we will be sheltered from all struggles. But when we are waiting on God and abiding in him, we can trust him with the end, stand firm, and rest in peace.

WHO IS YOUR ENEMY?—PSALM 27:12

David's enemies wanted to destroy him and spoke falsely against him. You might have enemies like that. Maybe you are waiting for vindication, have been falsely accused, or have someone seeking to intentionally harm you in some way. Or maybe no one is intentionally seeking to harm you, but neither are they concerned with your welfare or how their actions negatively impact you. Pray about those things! Like David, you can bring your fears before the Lord and ask for his protection.

In my experience, those types of enemies have never been the problem. Maybe you're the same. Maybe you would even struggle to name one person who could legitimately be thought of as an enemy. Perhaps your community is waiting alongside you, longing for the same resolution you desire. Maybe you aren't waiting for rescue so much as the filling of an unfulfilled longing or realization of a lifelong dream or even feeling unsettled because you are transitioning to the next season of life. So, maybe all this talk of enemies and opposition seems irrelevant to you. But is it?

Though we might be without earthly enemies, none of us is without any enemy. Not only do we contend with our own sinful nature and the pressures of a sinful worldly system, but we also have a spiritual enemy. We are called to humble ourselves before God, pray against temptation, and be aware of the schemes of Satan (Matthew 6:13; 1 Peter 5:6–11). First Peter 5:8 says, "Be sober-minded; be watchful. Your adversary the devil prowls around like a roaring lion, seeking someone to devour." And Ephesians 6:10–12 says, "Finally, be strong in the Lord and in the strength of his might. Put on the whole armor of God, that you may be able to stand against the schemes of the devil. For we do not wrestle against flesh and blood, but against the rulers, against the authorities, against the cosmic powers over this present darkness, against the spiritual forces of evil in the heavenly places." Part of waiting on God is being aware of spiritual reality, asking him for protection, and walking in the strength he provides.

SPIRITUAL WARFARE

How do we walk in this strength? Like most things, it is a habit we continually build. Notice how God's armor includes protection for the head in salvation. I often think of this as God protecting my mind with the truth of the gospel. I think about the call to take my thoughts captive (2 Corinthians 10:5) and to "be transformed by the renewal of your mind" (Romans 12:2). The breastplate of righteousness reminds me that my righteousness depends on Christ who took on my sin and gave me his righteousness (2 Corinthians 5:21). It also reminds me that the Holy Spirit is sanctifying me, growing me in Christlikeness and righteousness (Romans 8:28–30; Philippians 1:6). The sandals make me think of being ready to stand firm or to move nimbly, all based on the realities of the gospel. I can stand or move based on God's call because the gospel is true, and I am secure in him.

The belt of truth reminds me that everything is bound up in truth. All this holds together because it is true, and I need to cling to truth to stand firm. The belt imagery often reminds me of Hebrews 12:1 and the call to "lay aside every weight, and sin which clings so closely, and let us run with endurance the race that is set before us." We toss aside that which deters, wrap our armor together in truth, and keep pressing on, "looking to Jesus, the founder and perfecter of our faith" (v. 2). The shield of faith reminds me to hold fast to what I know to be true and to respond to the attacks of the enemy or the deceit of the world with trust in God (Matthew 4:1–11).

The sword of the Spirit reminds me that God's Word is powerful (Isaiah 55:10–11; 2 Timothy 3:16–17). I need to know it and let the Holy Spirit bring it to mind. God's Word is truth in which I can stand confident and by which I can dispel lies. Scripture declares the character and work of God, reminding me that my hope rests in his unchanging nature. The Bible is not mere instruction, but God's revelation of himself to humanity through language. It tells us the overarching narrative of history, who God is, what he does, who we are, and how we are to live. It gives us historical accounts of God's faithfulness such that we can trust in his present and future promises. It reminds us that Satan is defeated, we are loved, and God is sovereign. It tells us how to live in response to the realities of who God is and what he does. How do we have the Word in mind? We do this by the normal means of Christian growth—regular Bible reading and intentional study, prayer, fellowship with other believers, worship of God, and obedience to his commands. When I'm habitually spending time with God and others, I am much better equipped to stand firm and wait well.

Can you recall a time that God's Word came alive for you? In my intense season of waiting, this piece of armor became especially meaningful to me. One day, I was particularly encouraged by commentary on 2 John 1:1–3. The passage says, "The elder to the elect lady and her children, whom I love in truth, and not only I, but also all who know the truth, because of the truth that abides in us and will be with us forever: Grace, mercy, and peace will be with us, from God the Father and Jesus Christ the Father's Son, in truth and love." The commentary pointed out the connection between truth and love, and the word *abide* always seemed to jump off the page to me (for obvious reasons). Silence filled the room, and tears filled my eyes as I sensed God putting it together for me—truth, love, abide; this is how I designed you. This is what you're about.

To explain, each of these three words is profoundly and personally meaningful. Presumably, truth matters to everyone, but I seem to have an extra high dose of concern for truth and accuracy, even from childhood. Deception and its often-corresponding manipulation irk me. In my current work as an editor, I consider myself "the truth police." Is that a little much? Love is central to the human experience and especially to our lives as believers. My church lives and regularly speaks about our desire to "love well," so I'm often thinking about love. But even in childhood, I had a deep sense of being loved and a corresponding depth of care for other people. I want people to feel seen and known, and I want them to know truth so they can live in freedom. I long for my life to be characterized by both the truth and love of Christ. *Abide*, of course, was right on theme with what God was teaching me throughout the year. In that simple greeting from John and the insight of the commentator, God showed me that the passions he's given me are deeply connected. He saw me in that moment and made sure I knew it. He was confirming for me that his design was on purpose and that he was doing good things. In the course of my normal life, and in a season where I needed affirmation, the Holy Spirit made the Word come alive and bolstered my soul.

Later, as I was struggling with walking into the new thing, God brought the Israelites' experience in Canaan to mind as a visual to encourage me to keep going. I wrote Numbers 14:7–9 and Joshua 1:6–9 on a notecard to remind myself to stand firm. My church's concurrent sermon series from 1 Samuel on Saul and David was readily applicable to my situation. Earlier sermons on the "I AM" statements of Jesus spoke directly to my situation and reminded me that God saw me, knew me, and was enough for me. When struggling with anger over feeling misunderstood, I recalled the reality of spiritual warfare and passages about not allowing bitterness to grow (Hebrews 12:14–15; Matthew 5:23–24; 18:15). So, rather than allow the issue to fester, I addressed it.

The sword of the Spirit is powerful, even when you don't realize you're in the midst of a specific battle. So, engage with God's Word regularly and expectantly. You might be surprised when it comes alive and how he'll use it. Allow yourself to be sanctified in it (John 17:17). It takes time to make its way into your heart. Regular exposure is needed for later connections. For me, an explosion of connections came after having read through the Bible in a year with the help of a podcast.[1] Books on which I've done in-depth studies tend to stick. Your time in the Word is not likely to feel earth-shattering or meaningful every day. But that daily exposure makes a huge difference in the long run. Some have explained it as similar to making a deposit in a bank account; it builds over time and bears fruit later. So, stick with it. Let God's Word form your heart and your mind. Not only will it deepen your relationship with God and shape your daily life, it will prove vital in spiritual battle.

Many point out prayer as the final piece of the armor of God. Paul writes, "praying at all times in the Spirit, with all prayer and supplication. To that end, keep alert with all perseverance, making supplication for all the saints" (Ephesians 6:18). Prayer is vital! And, as I've mentioned before, a big enough topic that it deserves its own chapter. So, you'll just have to wait a bit longer for more.

STANDING FIRM—PSALM 27:13

After praying for protection, David declares confidence in the Lord: "I believe that I shall look upon the goodness of the LORD in the land of the living!" (Psalm 27:13). Though his prayer has expressed real fear and even doubt, David knows to whom he is praying. He has absolute trust that God is who he says and that he is good. Some versions include, "I would have despaired unless …" (NASB 1995). Had David not trusted in God, he would have been hopeless. If he thought God did not care or could not deliver him, he would have felt destitute. But he does trust God, so he is confident he will see God's goodness in the present—"in the land of the living."

---

1. Tara-Leigh Cobble's *The Bible Recap* was this helpful tool for me. You can find out more about it here: https://www.thebiblerecap.com/.

Notice that, given the tenor of the rest of this psalm, David's focus is not merely temporal. David has been clear that his foremost desire is a relationship with God. David's ultimate security is not in his circumstances, whether his enemies are surrounding him and defaming him or whether he is experiencing victory. His trust is in God. That challenges me. Does it challenge you? I wonder how often I wait for circumstantial change to feel secure or settled. It's easy to fall for the lie that the resolution to whatever it is we are waiting for will satisfy our souls, even when we know that's not true. How often do we find ourselves saying, "If only ... then ... ?" Or think life will start once whatever it is we are waiting for happens? I've found myself there before, with relationships, jobs, and even the progression of my dad's disease. Perhaps the rudest awakening was falling headfirst for the lie that one day I would arrive at this magical thing called adulthood and life would be steady from there.

Time after time, circumstances change, and they never satisfy for long. Our hope can never be in a specific circumstance or another person. We learn contentment in any and every situation by trusting in Christ (Philippians 4:11–13) and digging a deep foundation in him (Luke 6:46–49). Only God is unchanging—he is the same always and forever. That means he is completely trustworthy and faithful. He'll never be in a bad mood or have an off day and mess up. This is why people refer to God using words like *rock, firm foundation, stronghold, fortress,* and *refuge* (1 Samuel 2:2; Psalm 18:2; 31:3; 92:15; 94:22; 144:2).

Even though our security does not rest in circumstances, we can trust that we will see God's goodness in our present. We can long for particular ends and have genuine hope that God will be faithful in any situation. The difference is perspective. When we come to understand that our deepest need is to abide in the Lord, he will be our stability in any and every circumstance. So, while we yearn for relational reconciliation, a dream career, spouse, child, home, changed loved one, release from suffering, or whatever else it is we're waiting for, we know the resolution to those things will not satisfy the deepest longings of our souls. We also know they are still good things, and we can bring our honest desires before the Lord. Luke 11:5–13 tells us as much. A similar passage in Matthew says it this way, "If you then, who are evil, know how to give good gifts to your children, how much more will your Father who is in heaven give good things to those who ask him!" (Matthew 7:11; see also Matthew 6:25–34; James 1:17–18).

I've come to believe that, when we get to the base of them, our deepest longings are things that reflect God's character and hint at the eternal longing he has put in our hearts. Healthy relationships, effectively using our giftedness, release from suffering, and the like are foretastes of the restored world to come. So, we are right to long for them. But we also need to remember that, in the present, these are temporal gifts and can never be our gods. So, we place our waiting before the God who is (Exodus 3:14). He always has been, he always will be, he is present with us now, and we will be with him in the future. We can give him our longings, trusting in his goodness, and desiring to delight in him and give him glory in all things. The more we do, the more we find satisfaction in simply abiding in him (John 17:20–26; Philippians 1:21–26; 3:13–14; 4:12–13; 1 John 1:1–4).

TAKE COURAGE—PSALM 27:14

After declaring his confidence that he will see God's goodness, David goes on to encourage his heart to be strong and wait for the Lord. He ends the psalm with, "Wait for the LORD; be strong, and let your heart take courage; wait for the LORD!" This reminds me of the multiple encouragements to "be strong" and "stand" in Ephesians 6:10–14. I also think of Isaiah 50:7: "But the LORD GOD helps me; therefore I have not been disgraced; therefore I have set my face like a flint, and I know that I shall not be put to shame." Waiting requires boldness, faith, courage, stamina, and endurance. Waiting is not passive or weak; it is hopeful, courageous, and effortful. Trusting in who God is gives us strength to endure in waiting.

Notice how David's waiting is for God, not for change. Even though David believes God will deliver him in his earthly circumstances, his hope is ultimately in God himself. He waits for Yahweh, not for what Yahweh will do. What an incredible perspective. The Greek root translated as *for* in verse 14 has a sense of motion toward.[2] David is directing his thoughts toward God. He is looking expectantly in God's direction. This is not a passive sitting around for God to act or inactivity until a circumstance changes. Rather, this is an active belief and intentional setting of his mind and heart in God's direction. He is looking for God and expecting him to be present. David is not waiting for things to change; he is waiting for God himself.

I wonder if I am like that in my waiting. Are my eyes not only open to but actively looking for what God is doing, believing he is working, he knows what is best, he is supremely able to do all things, and he loves me fully? Circumstances can easily cloud our vision. The "tyranny of the urgent," the pain of a present hardship, the depth of longing for change, and the frustration of stagnation can cause us to lose focus. We are easily tempted to give up or try to force our way apart from God's timing. I've found that when I focus less on the situation I want to change and more on God and what he's doing, my circumstances come into perspective. I become less concerned about the specific reso-

---

2. "H413 - 'ēl - Strong's Hebrew Lexicon (esv)." Blue Letter Bible, accessed April 6, 2024, https://www.blueletterbible.org/lexicon/h413/esv/wlc/0-1/.

lution and more focused on character growth. I remind myself more of God's character and look to see it in action in the present. If resolution is not coming in my time and my way, it must be because God has something even better (Ephesians 3:20–21). This perspective can turn waiting into a fun adventure. What will God do? What is he doing now? It becomes a mystery where we get to be on the lookout for all the ways God is working.

As with any adventure, it takes courage. Perhaps this is why David concludes Psalm 27 with an exhortation to "be strong, and let your heart take courage." Waiting is not for the faint of heart. But you, my friend, can trust that "The LORD is the everlasting God, the Creator of the ends of the earth. He does not faint or grow weary; his understanding is unsearchable. He gives power to the faint, and to him who has no might he increases strength. Even youths shall faint and be weary, and young men shall fall exhausted; but they who wait for the LORD shall renew their strength; they shall mount up with wings like eagles; they shall run and not be weary; they shall walk and not faint" (Isaiah 40:28–31).

CHAPTER 7

LIVING IN THE PRESENT—
PRAYER

You've waited, and we made it to the chapter on prayer! We've learned some specifics about waiting from David's prayer in Psalm 27, and now we'll explore some more general concepts on waiting before focusing more specifically on abiding. Following David's example, we'll start with prayer.

Prayer is crucial always. In fact, prayer is one of the most powerful things believers can do. Why do I believe this? The Bible tells me so. First Thessalonians 5:16–18 says, "Rejoice always, pray without ceasing, give thanks in all circumstances; for this is the will of God in Christ Jesus for you." And Philippians 4:5–7 says, "The Lord is at hand; do not be anxious about anything, but in everything by prayer and supplication with thanksgiving let your requests be made known to God. And the peace of God, which surpasses all understanding, will guard your hearts and your minds in Christ Jesus" (compare with 1 Peter 5:6–7). James 5:16 says, "The prayer of a righteous person has great power as it is working." Ephesians 6:18 concludes the description of God's armor that we are to take up with, "praying at all times in the Spirit, with all prayer and supplication." Hebrews 4:14–15 talks about Jesus as our High Priest. Verse 16 encourages, "Let us then with confidence draw near to the throne of grace, that we may receive mercy and find grace to help in time of need." Prayer matters!

Building regular habits of prayer in our lives is key to abiding. As such, it's also key in our waiting. As children of God, we are invited to come to him in prayer—not just sometimes but always. We are to be in a spirit of prayer always. Prayer is part of our spiritual protection. It is how we receive comfort from God. It is how we come to him for wisdom (James 1:5). To think that we have ready access to the God of the universe is astounding. Perhaps even more incredible is the truth we learn in Romans 8:26: "Likewise the Spirit helps us in our weakness. For we do not know what to pray for as we ought, but the Spirit himself intercedes for us with groanings too deep for words." Not only does the Holy Spirit enable our prayers (Ephesians 6:18), he prays for us!

Jesus prayed extensively for his followers—including you and me—in John 17. Hebrews 7:24–25 tells us that "he holds his priesthood permanently, because he continues forever. Consequently, he is able to save to the uttermost those who draw near to God through him, since he always lives to make intercession for them." Jesus prays for us! Of course, Jesus also set the example for our prayer lives. As I pointed out in Chapter 4, Luke 5:16 says Jesus "would withdraw to desolate places and pray." Jesus communed regularly with the Father (Luke 3:21; 6:12; 9:18, 28–29), and we need to as well. Jesus also gave his disciples a model for how to pray (Luke 11:1–13) and even "told them a parable to the effect that they ought always to pray and not lose heart" (Luke 18:1).

SPECIFIC PRAYER

We desperately need time with God in prayer, and he invites us to it. The nitty-gritty theology of how and why prayer works is complex and debatable. Suffice it to say, we know God calls us to pray, we know God works through prayer, and we know God shapes and changes us through prayer. We pray out of obedience and in dependence on God. But what we sometimes miss is how prayer tunes us into what God is doing. If we are waiting for God—looking expectantly to him —but we're not praying, how will we notice what he's doing?

This is a reason to pray specifically and regularly. Two major illustrations from my own life come to mind. In my mid-twenties, I took a Bible study on spiritual armor that challenged the group to pray regularly and specifically about one big item in our lives. For me, it was my relationship with my mom. I was late to differentiating myself from my parents, so what many daughters and mothers go through in their teen years, I went through in my twenties. My mom and I simply were not connecting. Neither of us liked it, but neither of us knew what to do about it. So, I prayed; I'm sure she did too. And God answered! My attention was on the issue, and I saw how he worked through counseling, how he prepared and refined my heart, and how he eventually used my sister to prompt a needed conversation. Those comments from my sister broke the ice, my mom and I had a heart-to-heart, and major healing ensued. I was ready and willing to own my portion and seek genuine healing because of the time I spent with God. I was looking for him to act, trusting that he would. When he did, everything was ready. My relationship with my mom remains deep and life-giving to this day. Certainly, there are many factors, but I think for both of us, it all began with prayer. God accomplished his work, we were attuned to it, and we get to praise him all the more because we know what he did.

More recently, I saw God use prayer in my employment. As I've shared in preceding chapters, the organization was experiencing growing pains. For me, things began with feeling unsettled—personally and professionally. Unsure of why, I prayed. Others prayed for me as well. The ensuing season of waiting and discovery—for me and the organization—has ultimately been fruitful. But it has not been easy or always pleasant! I'll spare you the details and just say that I spent months on an emotional roller coaster of frustration, jubilation, questioning, waiting, seeing God move, seeing my sin, feeling stuck, feeling hopeful, and everything in between. My prayers reflected this emotional rollercoaster, along with many requests for wisdom, integrity, and circumstantial change. I prayed for daily conversations, for broad changes in the organization, for others in the organization, and for changes in myself. For months, it seemed like God was not moving. But he was revealing things to me about myself. That included the gifts and passions he's given me, which would not have been evident without what felt like a delay. It also included the greater needs of the organization, which, again, would not have been evident otherwise. He also revealed my sinful tendencies when frustrated, and he provided an opportunity for repentance and a chance to respond differently when I was frustrated later on. He showed me my utter dependence on him. Several times, I told others that I did not feel mature enough for the situation, but God kept equipping me and growing me. He also allowed tests that helped me see the fruit of things he had worked out in me previously. I had matured from years ago, and getting to see that was exciting. Plus, seeing that fruit gave me perspective on the current situation. Knowing how God had used the past to prepare me for the present helped me see how God would use the present to prepare me for the future. I began to see the situation as training rather than as a hardship to endure or escape (Hebrews 12:7–11).

Do you see hardship as training? This was an important paradigm shift for me. A leadership book highlighted the concept, but I think it was because I was praying that I could adopt and maintain the perspective. As I brought the desires of my heart to the Lord and explored the passions he placed in me, I could see how God was using the current situation to prepare and equip me. The waiting was a time of refining and teaching. Exposure of my sinful tendencies means I can be more intentional about not carrying those attitudes and actions forward. Knowing the circumstances that most triggered my sin means I can be more alert to temptation. Clarifying what matters to me and why helps me invest in the right things. Observing how people function together and how the "textbook instructions" for leadership play out in real life means I'm better able to serve in the various roles I occupy. Seeing community and collaboration in action grows my appreciation of others as well as my understanding of groups. I needed to grow in compassion, understanding, patience, and genuine appreciation of diversity in others. These attitudes matter for any interaction with people. My trust in God grew as I watched him orchestrate events and work in and through others. He didn't need me to make things happen or be anyone's savior. He's at work in everyone's life, not just mine; he is able to accomplish all things. I needed training to loosen my grip on control and pride. My amazement at who God is and what he does increased, and I could more readily rest in the reality that he will bring about his good purposes in his perfect timing and way. Some of these lessons are quickly applied; others I'm storing away for later, trusting that God wastes nothing and this season will continue to bear fruit in future calls.

God has a pattern of working in the waiting in the lives of his people (consider the training God did in Moses during his forty years as a shepherd in Midian or what David learned by serving Saul and while on the run). Waiting doesn't just strengthen our relationship with God, it's often a time of refining and intentional training for the next thing. Many times, it's in the waiting that our character is forged and our skills are honed. I wonder if you might see your season of waiting as training. What would change for you if you saw your struggles as formative and fruitful, much like a good workout? How is God using this season to shape you to be more like him? What might he be doing now to prepare you for what's ahead? What skills are you learning that you will need later? These are good questions to bring to God and process through prayer.

Prayer not only facilitated a change of perspective about how God was equipping me for the future, but it was also meaningful in noticing what he was working on in the present circumstance. Because I was praying and wanted to submit to God, I was on the lookout for where and how he was working. Yes, I still prayed for it to be over, but since God did not provide a way out, I started to open my eyes to what he was doing through the situation. He was doing good things! At one point, his answers were simply unmistakable, so much so that it was nearly comical. God's message to me was on repeat everywhere I looked, and the way forward was paved. Because I had been praying, I was attuned to the ways God was directing me and affirming that call. Others were praying for me and encouraging me. When I equivocated on decisions, I could look back to see all the events line up and be reminded that God's call had been clear. Were I not praying, I may not have stayed the course. I might not have noticed how God was directing each event and my steps so clearly. Had others not been praying, they might not have recognized the prompting from the Holy Spirit to give me the affirmation and encouragement I needed.

Because God is who he is, the timing of my changes coincided perfectly with things God was doing in others' lives too. It all worked together for individual and collective good. Because I was praying, I noticed those details. The details continued to affirm the call and thus increased my confidence. Each new detail I saw demonstrated God's faithfulness and deepened my awe. It began to feel like an adventure to see what God would do next. No longer was I merely waiting for something to change; I was genuinely expectant, almost on the edge of my seat, to see what God was orchestrating.

And it wasn't just about my job. God had awakened other dreams. It was in the midst of a particularly tense time at work that I spoke to the women's group I mentioned in the introduction. Per their request, the topic was Psalm 27:14. Did I say God's message to me was on repeat? A few weeks later, I attended a writing conference put on by a family friend, largely to see if I could be a coach to others and not at all for my own writing. Writing a book was nowhere on my radar, but here we are! I also recognized that I wanted to be more involved in women's ministry to help other women know and love God and live out their designs. In my mind, that was something years away, and, to be honest, maybe even some-what of a pipe dream.

Unbeknownst to me, around the same time, God was arranging things for the women's ministry deacon at my local congregation to relocate to be near her children and grand-children. She and her husband had known they wanted to move eventually but thought it would be years away. It was after God had given me unease at my job, after he kept doors closed to what I thought I wanted to do, after he stirred the desire in me to do more women's ministry, after he prompted me to fully step back from being an organizational change agent at work, and after he was showing me what that step-ping back was prompting for others that I heard about this move. A few weeks later, I was invited to step into the volun-teer women's ministry role at my church. Were it not for those months of refining and honing passion, all mediated through prayer, I would not have seen this as God's clear answer to the passions he was stirring and the places he was providing to use them. God was inviting me to use leadership giftings, to collaborate, and to have more opportunity to love and serve the women of my church. It was not what I had been expecting, but God's work was too obvious to deny. God opened the door, and because I and so many others had been praying, I knew to step through it.

Waiting requires prayer! There is simply no way to look for God expectantly, to be still before him, to know when he is calling us to move, or to boldly step out in faith when we do not know what will result if we are not coming to him in prayer. Ephesians 3:20–21 always comes to mind in this: "Now to him who is able to do far more abundantly than all that we ask or think, according to the power at work within us, to him be glory in the church and in Christ Jesus throughout all generations, forever and ever. Amen." I've heard this used to explain prayer. We pray specifically but also for God's will to be done because he has better plans. In essence, we can be honest with our needs and desires. Rather than "but thy will be done" as a cop-out in case our prayer feels unanswered, it's a call to say, "but your will is better." In short, "But if that's not your plan, blow my socks off with whatever your plan is." I can attest that he does! Never in my wildest dreams would I have imagined all that he would do in my life or the people around me. But I prayed. Because I did, I saw. And that seeing caused me to rejoice.

Perhaps even better, since I'd asked others to pray for me, they got to rejoice with me as well. It wasn't just me being in awe of each little detail God worked out; I shared those details with others. They knew the journey, so they got to be in awe of God too. He had answered their prayers! Sharing how God was working deepened my faith and heightened my joy. We get to see so much more of what God does when we come together in prayer. When we pray for others, our view is not limited to God's work in our own lives. We get to see the broader perspective, and that gives us a bigger view of God's faithfulness. Of course, it also deepens our bonds with one another. Prayer for one another is one of my favorite things about the family of God. It builds our sibling bonds and our understanding of our Father—all empowered by the Holy Spirit because of Jesus. Prayer is a key way we can be in union with God and with one another.

PRAYER AND COMMUNITY

Prayer is an incredibly practical way to share in one another's burdens (Galatians 6:2). Each of us is fully reliant on God. The best way we can help others is to bring them before the throne of the God who knows them, loves them, and can provide exactly what they need. When we pray for others, we invest in their lives. God uses prayer to grow our love for others. It is nearly impossible to pray for another's good and growth without becoming invested in it yourself. Something special happens when we pray for others and when we pray together. We become intertwined, not merely watching one another's lives, but genuinely living life together. Prayer is part of how we wait for God together.

Of course, this requires that we ask others to pray for us and that we offer to pray for others. This can feel intimidating. Likely, we've all been in small groups where the only requests people shared were for someone else, a missionary, or a health need. That's natural. But let's challenge ourselves to deeper things. We can and should pray for daily needs (Matthew 6:11), but the prayers we see most in the Bible relate to spiritual growth (John 17; Ephesians 1:16–23; 3:14–19; Philippians 1:3–11; Colossians 1:9–14). Pray for one another to know God, to be transformed into Christlikeness (Romans 8:28–30), to have renewed minds (Romans 12:1–2), to have relational unity and wholeness (Ephesians 4:1–3; Romans 12:16), to walk in freedom from sin (James 5:16), to live in contentment and strength (Philippians 4:12–13), and to have comfort in suffering (James 5:13; 2 Corinthians 1:3–7). Pray for those in leadership, "that we may lead a peaceful and quiet life, godly and dignified in every way" (1 Timothy 2:2). Pray for those who don't know Christ to come to saving faith (1 Timothy 2:3–5) and for people to speak God's Word with boldness (Ephesians 6:19–20). Pray for things like humility, forgiveness, and love of others. Pray for spiritual growth and the fruit of the Spirit to be evident (Galatians 5:22–25). Pray for spiritual protection and strength (Ephesians 6:10–18; 1 Peter 5:8–9).

In short, pray for the things we know are God's will for us as his children and for those who do not yet know him. Jesus told his disciples, "Whatever you ask in my name, this I will do, that the Father may be glorified in the Son. If you ask me anything in my name, I will do it" (John 14:13–14). And Psalm 37:4–5 says, "Delight yourself in the LORD, and he will give you the desires of your heart. Commit your way to the LORD; trust in him, and he will act." The more we know God, the more our hearts are shaped to desire what he desires. We pray in accordance with his will, trusting he will act in his good time and way. This will is not just an esoteric spiritual ideal but a real change in our hearts and lives. It is about relationships, about his kingdom purposes, about living out his desires for us in our specific contexts and seasons, about the body of Christ functioning as one (John 17:20–21), and together being a light to the world (Matthew 5:14–16). It's about us knowing God, seeing him at work, and giving him praise.

The Bible makes it obvious that God cares about the one. He works in the lives of real individuals in real ways. He cares about practical details like making an axe head float so borrowed property wouldn't be lost (2 Kings 6:1–7) and supplying food to those who are hungry (Matthew 14:13–21). He cares about things like restoring dignity (Matthew 9:20–22). All of these are details that work into his larger redemptive purposes and plans. Your life is no exception. So, bring him real needs, both for today and for eternity (Matthew 6:25–34). Trust that, as humans "who are evil, know how to give good gifts to your children, how much more will your Father who is in heaven give good things to those who ask him!" (Matthew 7:11). "He who did not spare his own Son but gave him up for us all, how will he not also with him graciously give us all things?" (Romans 8:32).

Prayer deepens our dependence on God. Prayer opens our eyes to the variety of ways he is working in our lives, in the lives of others, and in the world at large. Prayer shapes our hearts. Prayer is not the last resort but the first (Psalm 127:1–2). So, pray! Look eagerly to see how God is working the details of today into the larger story of your life and the larger story of his work in the world. Rejoice in each answer you see. Open your eyes to see the answers you didn't expect. Persist when you are uncertain because we "ought always to pray and not lose heart" (Luke 18:1). You might never see the final results of your prayers (Hebrews 11:39–40; 1 Peter 1:10–12). But you can rest assured that if you are in Christ, you are God's beloved child, and you can trust that he is a faithful, good, and wise Father. So, pray, seek, and wait expectantly for God. Do this not only for yourself but for others, and invite others to pray for you as well.

CHAPTER 8

LIVING IN THE PRESENT— GRIEF

A world of waiting is a world of grief. Recalling the past, yearning for the future, and living in the present won't change that. Loss is a pervasive reality in our lives. Even though we know we're living in the in-between and the final redemption that awaits is good beyond our imaginations, loss stings deeply. Death remains certain; and even with hope in Christ, it still hurts. Yet our grief is not related to mortality alone. We feel loss over broken relationships, misunderstandings, injustice, squashed dreams, unfulfilled longings, loneliness, disease, suffering, and more. We have a deep sense that things are not as they should be, and thus we grieve. What are we to do with all of this? Abide!

As you know by now, abiding is the only effective way to live. But it's also the only way we can truly and fully grieve. The current reality of death, with all its side effects, means things are not as they should be. Death, suffering, injustice, broken relationships, and heartache of all kinds exist only because humanity at large is not in a right relationship with God. These are all results of the fall. It is right to grieve what is wrong with this world. Genesis 3 is tragic. Sin brought death and brokenness, so much so that God the

Son took on human flesh, forever identifying himself with humanity, to bring redemption. This price of rescue is beyond our full comprehension, but it is one God willingly paid. He knew what would happen when he spoke the world into existence, and he chose to do it anyway. Jesus endured the cross "for the joy that was set before him" (Hebrews 12:2). From the eternal perspective, we know death is a defeated foe (1 Corinthians 15:56–58). We know a day is coming when "death shall be no more" (Revelation 21:4; also see Revelation 20:14). Instead of diminishing the emotions we feel about death and all its side effects, these realities affirm and even enhance them. God does not take brokenness lightly. When we grieve what is broken in our world, we connect with the heart of God. When we understand the depth of the destruction, we better appreciate the depth of the restoration God gives to all who put their trust in him.

God is the only one big enough to hold the full depth of our emotions over loss. He knows the truth of brokenness in far deeper ways than we do. We only know life in a fallen world. Yes, that fallen world still includes so much beauty and joy—glimpses and tastes of God's goodness. But God knows the fullness of his beauty, majesty, and glory. He knows what life truly is and just how desperately the world needs him. He knows the magnitude of all that has been lost. We can give full vent to our grief in the presence of God. Consider Jesus who wept over Lazarus (John 11:35). He entered into grief because death is awful, even when resurrection is a soon reality. Hebrews 4:14–16 encourages us, "Since then we have a great high priest who has passed through the heavens, Jesus, the Son of God, let us hold fast our confession. For we do not have a high priest who is unable to sympathize with our weaknesses, but one who in every respect has been tempted as we are, yet without sin. Let us then with confidence draw near to the throne of grace, that we may receive mercy and find grace to help in time of need." Draw near to God in your grief.

The Bible gives us multiple examples of this. Think of Hannah who "was deeply distressed and prayed to the LORD and wept bitterly" (1 Samuel 1:10). She was praying silently yet moving her lips, and the priest thought she was drunk! She told him, "I am a woman troubled in spirit. I have drunk neither wine nor strong drink, but I have been pouring out my soul before the LORD" (v. 15). Consider Jeremiah, the "weeping prophet," who wrote the book of Lamentations. There is an entire category of psalms known as the psalms of lament.

Psalm 42:1–4 says,

> As a deer pants for flowing streams,
>   so pants my soul for you, O God.
> My soul thirsts for God,
>   for the living God.
> When shall I come and appear before God?
> My tears have been my food
>   day and night,
> while they say to me all the day long,
>   'Where is your God?'
> These things I remember,
>   as I pour out my soul:
> how I would go with the throng
>   and lead them in procession to the house of God
> with glad shouts and songs of praise,
>   a multitude keeping festival.

This is a depiction of grief. Pour out your heart before the Lord. Allow the tears. Whether you are someone who experiences big emotions or is more emotionally reserved, there is space for you in God's presence. There is no right way to pour out your heart before him. You might be like Hannah who prays so vehemently that people mistake it as drunkenness. Perhaps you are like me and sometimes cry with guttural heaves too deep to even produce tears. Maybe you rarely cry, and you accept loss with relative ease. Maybe it's mostly intellectual for you. Perhaps you feel more angry than sad. Whatever the case, God sees and knows your heart (Psalm 56:8; 139:1–6). So, pour it out to him.

COMMUNITY IN GRIEF

Don't draw near to God only, draw near to community. A major gift of being a child of God is being included in his family. As believers, we have brothers and sisters in Christ with whom we share in life. Part of that is sharing our grief. Romans 12:15 says, "Rejoice with those who rejoice, weep with those who weep." Clearly, this requires cooperation on both parts. We need to be willing to tell others of our grief. And we need to be willing to sit in another's grief. This is all part of bearing one another's burdens (Galatians 6:2) and loving each other with the love of Christ (John 13:34–35). We need not grieve in isolation.

Have you ever cried in someone else's presence? As much as I feel things deeply, this is something I find myself trying to avoid, at least when it comes to crying about my pain in the presence of friends. My face cannot tell a lie, so it's obvious to others when I'm sad or hurt. But usually, when I tear up, I try to pull out of my emotions and go into my intellect to stay in a more factual exchange. Thankfully, I'm learning something new. In my concentrated season of waiting, my defenses failed. A friend casually asked me about my dad, and I barely got through the first word in explaining the situation before my throat closed with tears. He graciously put his arm on my shoulder and sat by my side while I continued to cry, completely unable to speak or stop the tears. To have my sadness witnessed, received, and shared did something deep for my heart. It still brings tears to my eyes today. I'm realizing there is power in allowing our hearts to be bare before our brothers and sisters in Christ so they can simply be with us in it.

Have you ever been in someone else's presence in their tears? This, too, is a powerful experience. When I've been in this situation, it feels so trusting, vulnerable, and even sacred. It taps into the deep places of our hearts, immediately moving us from solely intellectual engagement to genuine heart connection. If they are grieving, we feel their loss and share in their pain. I find that tearful exchanges are often part of relational reconciliation. I've had many difficult conversations in my life where I've expressed the pain that I've felt and apologized for the pain I've caused. Often, both I and the other person have had teary eyes. This allows for heart connection, which is where the mending is needed.

Have you ever had someone else cry for you, or have you cried for them? This, too, can be incredibly powerful. I hope to never forget the way a counseling professor described sometimes crying with clients as a way to recognize the situation. Sometimes her clients did not cry, but she would because the situation needed to be grieved. When we enter into another person's sadness, we share in their burden. We also share in the heart of God. Jerusalem did not recognize Jesus or know what was coming, but he did, and he wept over them (Luke 19:41–44). Whether in their presence or not, it is okay to cry for others. The sadness does not have to be our own to feel the weight.

For my non-criers out there, does it sound like I'm a little crazy and just advocating for a giant crying party? Let me assure you that while such a thing might be helpful for some, that is not what I'm promoting. What I am saying is that God has given us other people. We are called to love one another and to share in life with one another (Romans 12:9–18; Galatians 6:2; Hebrews 10:24–25; 1 John 4:7). We image God to others and are tangible conduits of his love. In Christ, we are brothers and sisters. So, share real life with each other. Enter into those familial relationships in real, family ways. Obviously, do so with wisdom and discernment. Like any family, the body of Christ has some "weird aunts" that aren't ready to share in this type of depth. The visible church also has some people who are not part of Jesus' family. And, of course, there are various levels of spiritual, emotional, and relational maturity. So, be wise. And know that human capacity is limited. It is normal to have different levels of relationships with different people. We cannot be everyone's best friend or favorite sister. We don't need to share our deepest heartaches with anyone and everyone. But we also cannot keep them to ourselves and expect to be okay; we can't expect others to be either.

When someone entrusts you with their heart, do your best to be willing to receive it. Also, remember that their grief is not yours to bear alone. Only God can bring comfort and healing. We simply share with one another in the moment. We are not rescuers, only Jesus is. As Paul wrote, "Blessed be the God and Father of our Lord Jesus Christ, the Father of mercies and God of all comfort, who comforts us in all our affliction, so that we may be able to comfort those who are in any affliction, with the comfort with which we ourselves are comforted by God" (2 Corinthians 1:3–4). We can only share the comfort we have received, and we can only do so by the strength of the Holy Spirit.

When we share grief in community, we share in the heart of God, love one another with his love, receive his comfort in unique ways, and participate in his work in one another's lives. We also do this through prayer. Grieving in community is not just about presence or tears, it's also about intentionally taking one another before the Lord. Praying with and for one another is powerful. It reminds us of our dependence on God and our desperate need for him. It reminds us that he is there, and he does see and care. Praying together shows us that we are not in this alone. Life is not just about me and God, or just about me and others, or just about me. It's about God, others, and me. Prayer is a tangible way we enter into this community.

Of course, there are other tangible ways as well. When my dad died, our family was surrounded by community. People visited him and us in the nursing home in his final days, they brought meals, sent cards, gave flowers and other gifts, provided paper goods to ease hosting out-of-town relatives, put together photos for the memorial slide show, came to the memorial service, cleaned up from the service, asked about us, shared memories of my dad, asked us to share memories, listened, checked in, invited us to do fun things, and continued to share in life. Community was so evident and present. They were not afraid to engage with our family. In fact, they were eager to do so, and they stayed the course. A few people did many, many things for us. But so very many people did one or two things. And you know what? Those things really added up. Your one card or one text or one email or one question really matters to those who are grieving.

Follow God's prompting and your unique gifting in how to best love others in grief. All the ways of sharing in grief are needed. Allow others to love you in God-directed ways when you are grieving. You need it, and they probably do too. Don't be afraid to engage, don't bear the load alone, and don't let your friends bear it alone either. Community is crucial for navigating grief. It is a comfort to have others surround you, and there is a special joy in being able to surround others who are grieving.

GOODNESS IN GRIEF

Grief is not merely something to be managed or navigated. Clearly, we do not want to wallow in devastation, but there is goodness in grief. We know grief connects us to the heart of God and one another. And yet, it is admittedly rather frightening to be willing to see the devastation of the fall and the stark reality in which we live. We might think we'd be better off ignoring it or at least downplaying it. But acknowledging the truth is never the wrong thing. It is because we know that we have a sovereign God who has provided rescue and who is completing his plans that we can acknowledge the desperation of our situation. Were he not real or good or rescuing, then maybe pretending would be a better idea. But he is real, and he loves you, and he has the victory.

As I alluded to earlier, I wonder if it is in more fully recognizing just how deeply death and all of its related features affect us that we come to a better understanding of what eternal life really is. Jesus said, "The thief comes only to steal and kill and destroy. I came that they may have life and have it abundantly" (John 10:10). Grieving the depth of the tragedy of death helps us more fully understand the inexplicable depth of the gift of life in Christ.

Not only does that give us greater cause to praise God, but it also gives us greater urgency to share the reality of eternal life with others. They may not see how broken the world is and how in need they are of restoration in God, but we do, and in seeing that reality, our love for those who are blinded by the deceit of Satan and of sin grows (2 Corinthians 4:4). In this, too, our hearts connect to the heart of God (Ezekiel 33:11; 2 Peter 3:9).

Grieve the losses—of all kinds. Take it all to the Lord. Share it with community. Understand just how broken, depraved, and desperate this world truly is. Wrestle with your unfilled longings and unmet expectations. Name the pain of your season of waiting. Grieve the things that have died and not yet been restored. Grieve the things you fear never will be. But grieve with hope (1 Thessalonians 4:13).

Remember Psalm 42:1–4? That's not where it ends. The

final verse says, "Why are you cast down, O my soul, and why are you in turmoil within me? Hope in God; for I shall again praise him, my salvation and my God" (v. 11). In verse 8, the psalmist confidently declares, "By day the LORD commands his steadfast love, and at night his song is with me, a prayer to the God of my life." In the depth of our pain, we still know the truth about God. And we are right to remind ourselves of it. We cry out to him because we know who he is. We do not belittle the hardships, but neither do we forget the truth.

The one who created the world perfectly will restore it to himself. He currently sustains it and us. Remember that "the Spirit helps us in our weakness. For we do not know what to pray for as we ought, but the Spirit himself intercedes for us with groanings too deep for words" (Romans 8:26). Cling to the truth that "the sufferings of this present time are not worth comparing with the glory that is to be revealed to us" (Romans 8:18) and that "in all these things we are more than conquerors through him who loved us" (Romans 8:37) and absolutely nothing can separate us "from the love of God in Christ Jesus our Lord" (Romans 8:38–39).

Be encouraged by 1 Corinthians 15:56–58: "The sting of death is sin, and the power of sin is the law. But thanks be to God, who gives us the victory through our Lord Jesus Christ. Therefore, my beloved brothers, be steadfast, immovable, always abounding in the work of the Lord, knowing that in the Lord your labor is not in vain."

You, my friend, are waiting in a world of grief. But you are waiting for God. Be expectant and hopeful. He will come, and, in fact, he is with you now. Abide in him with confidence!

CHAPTER 9

TRANSITION

It often feels like waiting never ends. In many ways, it doesn't. Within the grander redemptive arc, we are living in the in-between. Within our lifetimes, we'll always be waiting for something. But specific seasons of waiting come to an end. Circumstantial resolution occurs with a good degree of regularity. What do you expect when it does? If you're like me, I expect relief, ease, a sense of freedom, and life feeling "right" again. Hopefully, you're not like me! Those expectations are unrealistic. Life doesn't become "right" suddenly just because that one thing changed. We still live in a fallen world, and it still impacts our daily lives even when those big issues feel resolved. Not only that, but we experience some level of loss when seasons change; even when we long for and rejoice in the new season, we might still grieve. Parents and newlyweds seem especially able to attest to this. Perhaps more easily overlooked, transition simply takes time. Someone once explained to me that humans aren't like toasters; we don't just plug into a brand-new environment or reality and turn on. There is an adjustment period to the new normal even when that newness is something for which you have longed and in which you are rejoicing.

This reality took me by surprise as my life season shifted. The things I'd been waiting on were moving. It was a new season, but I didn't know how to keep up or adjust. There wasn't a new rhythm, and nothing felt normal. Emotionally, I shifted from excited for the new, to overwhelmed at what it would look like, to grieving the pain of the prior waiting period, to rejoicing in all the ways God was evident, to questioning my perceptions about everything, to doubting my competence, to remembering that God equips, to stunned gratitude for all God had done, to trepidation about the unknowns ahead, to ... you get the picture! Change, even good change, is exhausting!

So, what do we do when the waiting is over? What do we do when some waiting is over and other waiting persists? You know by now—abide! The only way to effectively endure and boldly walk into what God calls us to is by the power of the Holy Spirit. When our world is awhirl, and even when it isn't, we cannot look to our circumstances or ourselves for peace. We can only keep looking to God for direction.

As I've mentioned in prior chapters, in my transition, the image of the Israelites entering Canaan became particularly meaningful for me. Again, mapping Bible stories onto our lives as if we're the people in those accounts and God will work the same way in our lives is not a good way to understand the Bible. But history, particularly biblical history, is instructive in understanding who God is and who we are (1 Corinthians 10:6; Hebrews 12:1–2). For many, a particular account becomes a special source of encouragement in a given life season. That's how God used the Israelites, and especially Joshua, for me. Earlier, I mentioned that obedience can be challenging when we have a temptation to "return to Egypt" or when there are "giants in the land" of what God is calling us into. It seems to me these temptations most often come in transition. In between one season and another, we aren't sure what to do, and we can feel a little lost.

The Israelites chose poorly when first presented with the spies' report of Canaan, and they suffered for it. But God protected them and brought their descendants into the land. I began to think about Joshua during those forty years. He had believed God and was willing to go into the land (Numbers 13—14), but he had to wait forty years to do so. He would become the leader of the people, and that time was preparatory for him as he assisted Moses. This preparation began before the Israelites' refusal. We find out in Exodus 24:13 that Joshua went up Mount Sinai with Moses. During the forty years, he continued as Moses' assistant. Exodus 33:11 says, "Thus the LORD used to speak to Moses face to face, as a man speaks to his friend. When Moses turned again into the camp, his assistant Joshua the son of Nun, a young man, would not depart from the tent." I wonder what God worked out in his heart and mind in that time of waiting.

As Joshua prepared for the transition into the new, God encouraged him with this:

> Be strong and courageous, for you shall cause this people to inherit the land that I swore to their fathers to give them. Only be strong and very courageous, being careful to do according to all the law that Moses my servant commanded you. Do not turn from it to the right hand or to the left, that you may have good success wherever you go. This Book of the Law shall not depart from your mouth, but you shall meditate on it day and night, so that you may be careful to do according to all that is written in it. For then you will make your way prosperous, and then you will have good success. Have I not commanded you? Be strong and courageous. Do not be frightened, and do not be dismayed, for the LORD your God is with you wherever you go.
>
> JOSHUA 1:6–9

In this, we see themes we've already touched on. Joshua is encouraged to remember God's past promise and to look ahead to the future. He is to meditate on God's Word, bathing his mind in the truth of who God is and allowing his heart to be shaped to rely on God and live according to his ways. He is called to obey and exhorted to have strength and courage. His hope is not about the circumstances but about God's presence.

I particularly appreciate the way Joshua is commanded to meditate on God's Word. In transition and in waiting, it's all too easy to fall for deception. The best defense against deception has always been truth. When we're transitioning, we need to stay grounded in the truth of who God is and what he does. Regular Bible reading and study is the best way to do this. *Meditate* in Joshua 1:8 carries with it the idea of murmuring and pondering.[1] Some have given the illustration of chewing the cud; the idea is that of continual rumination. God's Word is to be always on his mind and even on his lips. The words in Joshua 1 were spoken to Joshua by God, and it is a command he is expected to carry out individually. But that does not mean Joshua stays courageous in isolation. Earlier God had used Moses to encourage the young man. In Exodus 17, God instructed Moses to write the account of Joshua's defeat of Amalek "as a memorial in a book and recite it in the ears of Joshua, that I will utterly blot out the memory of Amalek from under heaven" (v. 14). Staying grounded in the truth of who God is has to do both with regularly reminding ourselves and allowing others to remind us. There are no substitutes for personal time with God or for the family of believers—and we need both.

Back to the Israelites. Deuteronomy 7 is another illumi-

---

1. "H1897 - hāgâ - Strong's Hebrew Lexicon (esv)." Blue Letter Bible, accessed October 26, 2024, https://www.blueletterbible.org/lexicon/h1897/esv/wlc/0-1/.

nating example. Moses gives the people instructions for entering into the Promised Land. For one, they were to "devote [the enemy nations] to complete destruction" (v. 2). This has to do with God's judgment on those evil nations (Genesis 15:16) and his making Israel into a holy nation. They were to remove the false gods to not be trapped in idolatry and to live as God's people instead (Deuteronomy 7:4–6). Though our idols might not be made of wood and stone, we are certainly tempted by the idols of the world around us (1 John 2:15–17). In transition, it is especially easy to seek comfort in things that are lesser or that will cause us to stumble. When we enter into new seasons, we need to be cognizant that we are not being shaped by our environment; instead, we need to be shaped by God. Pay attention to where you find your sense of security and identity. Be mindful of your routines, speech, and thoughts. Are there inputs you need to remove or things you need to avoid? A new situation brings with it new temptations, even things we've never encountered before, and sometimes are completely unexpected. New situations also bring new ideas. We need to think critically and only adopt what lines up with truth. Ask God to examine your heart and help you see if any idols need to be destroyed or if there are any traps you need to avoid.

After instructing the Israelites how to clear the land and keep from following false gods, Moses specifically addresses fear: "If you say in your heart, 'These nations are greater than I. How can I dispossess them?' you shall not be afraid of them but you shall remember what the LORD your God did to Pharaoh and to all Egypt, the great trials that your eyes saw, the signs, the wonders, the mighty hand, and the outstretched arm, by which the LORD your God brought you out" (Deuteronomy 7:17–19). When facing fear in transition, they were to remember the past and stand firm in who God is.

The instruction becomes particularly pertinent to transition when we read, "You shall not be in dread of them, for the LORD your God is in your midst, a great and awesome God. The LORD your God will clear away these nations before you little by little. You may not make an end of them at once, lest the wild beasts grow too numerous for you. But the LORD your God will give them over to you and throw them into great confusion, until they are destroyed" (Deuteronomy 7:21–23). God would not give them more than they were ready for, and he would be with them! He did not release them from waiting to launch them unprotected, unprovided for, and alone into something overwhelming. No! He would continue to walk with them each step and provide the victory.

Again, we should not map biblical accounts onto our lives. But it is safe to say that God remains faithful to us today. He does not launch us out of a waiting season on our own into something filled with giants that will overwhelm us. Just as he was with us in the waiting, he is with us in the transition. Second Peter 1:3–4 gives this encouragement: "His divine power has granted to us all things that pertain to life and godliness, through the knowledge of him who called us to his own glory and excellence, by which he has granted to us his precious and very great promises, so that through them you may become partakers of the divine nature, having escaped from the corruption that is in the world because of sinful desire." If God is with us, we need not fear. We have all we need in transition. We need simply to abide.

TIPS FOR TRANSITION

How can we proactively live in this truth, specifically in transition? Second Peter 1 goes on to say, "For this very reason, make every effort to supplement your faith with virtue, and virtue with knowledge, and knowledge with self-control, and self-control with steadfastness, and steadfastness with godliness, and godliness with brotherly affection, and brotherly affection with love" (vv. 5–7). This sounds a lot like growing in our love and knowledge of God, obeying him, loving others, and participating in community. Are you catching on to some similar themes when it comes to abiding?

For me, my thoughts and emotions are among the biggest hurdles in transition. Maybe that's because my new seasons have yet to be in new locations, so I'm usually just trying to get my perspective to catch up and not having to learn a lot of new people, responsibilities, traffic patterns, stores, etc. There are helpful tricks for those things, but I imagine thoughts and emotions are foundational no matter what our transition looks like. So, how can we help ourselves?

One habit is to regularly examine our thoughts (2 Corinthians 10:3–5). In doing so, we can know what thoughts we need to get rid of, replace them with something else, and then rehearse the truth so that unhelpful thoughts are less likely to intrude to begin with (Romans 12:1–2). For me, my emotions often follow my thoughts. The more I'm immersed in truth and focusing on who God is, the less overwhelmed and unstable I feel.

Similarly, regularly examine your emotions and bring them to God. What are those emotions indicating about your current experience? Are you lashing out in anger at the barista because you're actually angry at God about your current situation? Or did you just not sleep well last night? Are you experiencing a relatively small loss as huge because it compounds the grief you're already carrying? Is the emotion showing you something deeper that needs to be processed? Is it based on something true or something false? Is it your emotion, or is it something you are carrying for or picking up from someone else? Is what you're feeling showing you that you need to change your schedule or something about the way you care for your body? Are you feeling something that is connecting you to the heart of God and his heart for the world?

Sometimes, just knowing what is going on in your heart and expressing it is very healing. For me, that often happens through prayer, specifically in writing out my prayers. It also happens in verbally sharing with others. Some people just need an "aha moment," alone or through verbal processing, to name the emotion, which can bring insight and lift the weight. How and when people examine and process emotions varies. Common ones I hear about are exercise, time outdoors, artwork, doing mindless tasks like taking a shower or driving, listening to music, talking with a friend, or even connecting with something in a story. The general idea is to be aware of what is going on in your mind and heart. Be open before the Lord. Ask him to expose what you need to see, and then trust him with it.

As an aside, our society seems to have an uncertain relationship with emotions, with some wanting to be emotionless and others believing every emotion is indicative of absolute truth. That's probably a little extreme, but you get the idea. Each of us experiences and expresses emotions in different ways. I seem to be a woman with big emotions that I often express with my words and my body. I'm learning to rejoice in this part of God's design. I'm also learning, as with everything in life, that I need to surrender my emotions to God. I cannot allow emotions to dictate my beliefs about reality or to drive my reactions. But I can experience them with the Lord and allow him to direct me. I see evidence of people doing just that throughout the Bible—Psalms, Lamentations, the Gospels' depictions of Jesus, and Paul's language in his letters. Emotions are a part of God's design of humanity and how we experience the world. The goal is not to be emotionless or to be emotion-filled. Running from emotion, denying uncomfortable feelings or less-than-godly thoughts, or even not allowing ourselves to deeply experience happy emotions, usually does not turn out well. Neither does pressing into every emotion, examining it to death, or living by it as truth.

What we do want is to be fully honest before God in heart, mind, and spirit. And we want all of those things to conform to who he is. We want to be ruled by his Spirit and his truth, bringing our entire selves to him. We can ask him to search us, know us, and lead us in his ways (Psalm 139:23–24).

As in every season of life, the community of believers remains important in transition. Other believers can remind us of truth (Ephesians 4:15, 29; 2 Timothy 2:2), share in our needs (Romans 12:13), help us turn away from sin and toward obedience (James 5:19–20), and encourage us to press on (1 Thessalonians 5:14). Perhaps one of the most challenging things about transition is that it often involves a change of community or shifts in individual relationships. Building community takes time, which is why we value that handful of lifelong friends so deeply. Invite the people already in your life to walk with you as you transition. Also, take the opportunity to invite new people in and to grow new relationships. In Christ, the sibling bond is a fact, so do your best to find other believers to walk by your side. Recognize that a time with less community can be a sweet time of deepening your relationship with the Lord. Some of us err on the side of not inviting other people in. Others of us err on the side of relying on people instead of on the Lord. In truth, we need both. Transition can be a good time to examine our relationships and submit them to the Lord. The key takeaway here is that you are not alone! God is always with you, and more than likely, other believers are ready to be with you too.

BIBLICAL ENCOURAGEMENT—PHILIPPIANS 4:4–9

Helpful guidance in transition is found in Philippians 4. Verses 4–7 say, "Rejoice in the Lord always; again I will say, rejoice. Let your reasonableness be known to everyone. The Lord is at hand; do not be anxious about anything, but in everything by prayer and supplication with thanksgiving let your requests be made known to God. And the peace of God, which surpasses all understanding, will guard your hearts and your minds in Christ Jesus."

Notice how rejoicing is something for always. Joy and gladness in the Lord persist because he doesn't change. Our foundation in him remains firm regardless of external circumstances. Our "reasonableness" is a "gentle spirit" (NASB) or "graciousness" (CSB) or "forbearance" (ASV). Resting in the Lord allows us to be tempered in our responses and fair with others. Knowing that Jesus is returning, we need not be anxious. And yet this life does come with many worries (John 16:33); we are called to take them to the Lord. Rather than stew on our anxious thoughts, we turn to him in prayer. We can bring our burdens to the throne of God, "casting all your anxieties on him, because he cares for you" (1 Peter 5:7). We can remind ourselves of the truth of who God is and what he has done. When we know God is both sovereign and good, we can rest in him.

Part of experiencing the peace of God is keeping a right perspective. Paul goes on to say, "Finally, brothers, whatever is true, whatever is honorable, whatever is just, whatever is pure, whatever is lovely, whatever is commendable, if there is any excellence, if there is anything worthy of praise, think about these things" (Philippians 4:8). We need to wash our minds in truth so we are not easily deceived by our world or overwhelmed by our circumstances. This is part of setting our "minds on things that are above" (Colossians 3:2). It is not a call to bury one's head in the sand or to dismiss the realities of hardship. Instead, it is a call to focus on what is of God. When we are clinging to him, we know he can and will get us through. When we turn our minds and hearts to him, we can see more clearly. And that helps us endure.

It is not only about our thoughts but what we do. Paul encourages the Philippians to follow his example (Philippians 4:9). James talks about being "doers of the word" (James 1:22).

Knowing the right things and focusing on beautiful things does no good if we do not act on those things (James 2:17). Part of abiding in Christ is believing him enough to follow what he says (John 15:10–11; 1 John 2:4–6). This is not about obedience to earn favor or working to prove something about ourselves. Rather, it is believing God's way is best. He is the way of life! We walk according to his ways, not only because he is worthy but because that is for our best. Wholeness comes as we continually grow in and obey God.

By nature, transition is unstable. But we serve a God who is unchanging. In setting our thoughts on the things of God, aligning our hearts to who he is, and living it out, we can experience peace even in chaos. When our waiting is over for a time, but our world feels like chaos, we continue to abide. We stand firm on the Rock of our salvation, remind ourselves of truth, keep walking as he calls us to do, and trust he is faithful. We navigate the transition the same way we do the rest of life—abiding in him.

CHAPTER 10

ABIDING—JOHN 15

Though specific seasons of waiting come to an end, and we successfully transition to new seasons, waiting is a persistent reality of life. Waiting in the general sense never ends, at least not this side of eternity. In part, because of this, abiding must be a lifelong habit. And yet, abiding is not only meant to enable effective waiting—abiding is a foretaste of eternity! Waiting lasts a lifetime, but abiding never ends. Humanity began in a garden where God walked (Genesis 3:8). In Jesus "the Word became flesh and dwelt among us" (John 1:14). Of the new heavens, new earth, and new Jerusalem, the apostle John heard a voice from heaven proclaim, "Behold, the dwelling place of God is with man. He will dwell with them, and they will be his people, and God himself will be with them as their God" (Revelation 21:3). Being with God and other believers is where the redemptive narrative of the Bible starts and where it culminates. Eternal abiding is our future, and it's also our present! So, let's dwell on what abiding actually is.

As established in Chapter 1, the word *abide* has to do with physically inhabiting a place, dwelling, enduring, and remaining present. Another way I think of abiding is being part of the fabric of something, almost like an intimate belonging. It is living, in the full sense, somewhere. We abide when we make our home in a place, when we find rest there, when we are refreshed there, and when we are our full selves there. We abide when we continue to endure, no matter what may come. When I talk about abiding in God, it means him living in you and you living in the reality of who he is. In Christ, the Holy Spirit has made you his dwelling place. We abide as we invest in the reality of our newness in Christ and our intimate connection with the Father. We abide as we are aware of the fullness of God and center our lives around him. He is not merely our priority; he is in us and our lives are in him.

John 15:1–17 is the first passage that comes to mind when I think about the word *abide*. It records Jesus speaking to his disciples on the night he was arrested to be crucified. Chapters 13 through 17 are powerful; I'd highly suggest you read through them to have a better understanding of the context and reminder of the depth of Jesus' incredible love, God's abundance, and the astounding nature of what it means to be rescued by the living God and invited into genuine relationship with him. I'll wait …

And I'll draw out the anticipation. Before we head to John 15, take a minute to linger on John 14:16–17: "And I will ask the Father, and he will give you another Helper, to be with you forever, even the Spirit of truth, whom the world cannot receive, because it neither sees him nor knows him. You know him, for he dwells with you and will be in you." The word *dwell* is from the same root as *abide* throughout John 15. Also notice John 14:20–21: "In that day you will know that I am in my Father, and you in me, and I in you. Whoever has my commandments and keeps them, he it is who loves me. And he who loves me will be loved by my Father, and I will love him and manifest myself to him." Then look at John 17:20–26. This is Jesus praying for future believers "that they may all be one, just as you, Father, are in me, and I in you, that they also may be in us, so that the world may believe that you have sent me" (v. 21). Jesus says, "Father, I desire that they also, whom you have given me, may be with me where I am, to see my glory that you have given me because you loved me before the foundation of the world" (v. 24).

Notice the relationship among the Trinity, the way believers are invited in, and the way believers are to be united together. Jesus' desire to be with us is evident. This all speaks to some incredible abiding! And it's not just a future hope; if you are in Christ, the Holy Spirit lives inside of you and will be with you forever. God himself abides in us. Jesus came to earth to dwell with people temporarily, but he has not abandoned his people; he is preparing a place so that we might be with him (John 14:2–3; Revelation 21:3). Abiding is God's idea, not ours. That we would abide in him is his desire for us. That he would invite us into this is a gift beyond words.

Notice how others are included. It is not just me abiding in God but us. And it is not just us and God but us and one another. First John 1:3–4 depicts this beautifully: "That which we have seen and heard we proclaim also to you, so that you too may have fellowship with us; and indeed our fellowship is with the Father and with his Son Jesus Christ. And we are writing these things so that our joy may be complete." Notice how fellowship with God leads to fellowship with other believers and how it all leads to joy.

In Christ, God is in you, and you are in him. You are also part of the family of believers (Romans 8:14–17, 29; Ephesians 4:1–6). Jesus' life, death, and resurrection were not only intended to atone for our sins and to reconcile us to God. He reconciles us to one another, making us into a new family (Ephesians 2:11–22; 1 Peter 2:9–10). And it's not just about forgiveness and sin either. Jesus brings fullness of life (John 10:10)! It begins with atonement and continues with abiding.

We are welcome to be at home—fully—with God. That's incredible!

As an aside, you might be noticing how the apostle John was particularly fond of writing about the themes of abiding and love. In his gospel, he referred to himself as "the disciple whom Jesus loved" (John 21:20, 24). I wonder if his complete confidence in Jesus' love for him had something to do with his abiding in Christ.

TEXT AND OVERVIEW—JOHN 15:1–17

With those thoughts in mind, let's see what we can learn from Jesus' words in John 15 about abiding. For your convenience, below are some especially pertinent portions:

> I am the true vine, and my Father is the vinedresser. Every branch in me that does not bear fruit he takes away, and every branch that does bear fruit he prunes, that it may bear more fruit ... Abide in me, and I in you. As the branch cannot bear fruit by itself, unless it abides in the vine, neither can you, unless you abide in me. I am the vine; you are the branches. Whoever abides in me and I in him, he it is that bears much fruit, for apart from me you can do nothing ... If you abide in me, and my words abide in you, ask whatever you wish, and it will be done for you. By this my Father is glorified, that you bear much fruit and so prove to be my disciples. As the Father has loved me, so have I loved you. Abide in my love. If you keep my commandments, you will abide in my love, just as I have kept my Father's commandments and abide in his love. These things I have spoken to you, that my joy may be in you, and that your joy may be full. This is my commandment, that you love one another as I have loved you ... No longer do I call you servants, for the servant does not know what his master is doing; but I have called you friends, for all that I have heard from my Father I

have made known to you. You did not choose me, but I chose you and appointed you that you should go and bear fruit and that your fruit should abide, so that whatever you ask the Father in my name, he may give it to you. These things I command you, so that you will love one another.

JOHN 15:1–2, 4–5, 7–12, 15–17

You're probably already picking up on a few things we've discussed before. God's Word is consistent, and he is faithful to remind us of the truths we need to know. So, if it sounds like I'm repeating myself in this book, it's probably because I am. But back to God reminding us of truth. Did you notice the expectant waiting on God? The Father is the vinedresser and Jesus is the vine—the branches are fully dependent on God, and he is faithful to produce the fruit. Did you see the importance of God's Word, prayer, obedience, and community? Did you see the way joy is linked? Much like David longed for God's presence more than his provision, abiding in Christ is about being with God, not just the fruit it produces. Even that fruit is a joining with God in his work; he invites us in and makes the fruit last. I love how consistent God is in his desires for his people and in his instructions. Let's take a deeper dive into these verses.

GOD'S WORK IN ABIDING—JOHN 15:1–3

Jesus does not understate our need for him or our position in him. He is the vine, we are the branches, and we can do nothing on our own. The only means by which our lives will generate meaningful fruit is to abide in Christ. The Father has a role in this, and as we saw in John 14, so does the Holy Spirit. Branches do not connect themselves to vines. In Christ, we are already connected (John 15:3). Yet we do need to abide to receive spiritual nourishment and have fruitful lives.

Notice how in John 15:2 the Father faithfully tends to the

branches. God does intentional work to mature, refine, and prune us. I'm not a gardener by any stretch of the imagination. The plants in my home were given to me and have managed to survive because of big windows, skylights, and their low-maintenance nature. But I understand the general concept of pruning—removing parts of the plant to best direct its growth. This includes taking away portions that are diseased or are otherwise hindering full fruitfulness. Plants that are never cut back don't do well. Pruning is a vital part of gardening. It's also a vital part of life. Hopefully, we're all pruning our schedules and pursuits of things that are impeding the right growth.[1]

When God prunes us, he is molding and shaping our character. He's conforming us to the image of Christ (Romans 8:29). Pruning looks like a lot of things. It might be a natural change of life season or maybe some lesson that God seems to keep emphasizing everywhere you go. It might also be a general trial or hardship that God will use (Romans 5:3–5; James 1:2–8). Or it might be more related to specific discipline. Hebrews 12 says God disciplines his children, "for our good, that we may share in his holiness. For the moment all discipline seems painful rather than pleasant, but later it yields the peaceful fruit of righteousness to those who have been trained by it" (vv. 10–11). Notice that the fruit comes later. I would argue that much of the waiting in our lives is God's work of pruning.

THE FRUIT OF ABIDING—JOHN 15:4–5, 8

Abiding always results in fruit, and it is the Holy Spirit who produces fruit in our lives (Galatians 5:22–23). We have an

---

1. Henry Cloud's *Necessary Endings: The Employees, Businesses, and Relationships That All of Us Have to Give Up in Order to Move Forward* (New York: Harper Business, 2010) is a helpful resource on this if you've never considered the concept.

active role in abiding, but just as we are saved by God's grace through faith, we are sanctified by God's grace through faith (Galatians 3:1–9). We cannot bear fruit by ourselves!

Have you ever gotten that mixed up? I have. For years, I lived in what I refer to as my "perfect box." In my mind, I had an image of what a Christian woman was supposed to be, and I sought to be that person. Needless to say, it didn't work! In his faithfulness, God destroyed my box. It was painful to recognize the depth of my need for him but also so freeing. Letting go of my ideals about what life was supposed to look like and my sense of control and pride in how my life would go took effort. But acceptance through performance is tenuous and false. Anyone who has been a people-pleaser knows the impossibility and insecurity of it. Anyone who has tried to earn another's love is familiar with the futility and the heartache.

The good news is that this is not the type of love our Father has for us. He isn't asking us to fit ourselves into a perfect box, especially one of our own making. He is pruning us and molding us in the security of his perfect love. He is completing his good work in us (Philippians 1:6), "for we are his workmanship" (Ephesians 2:10). God's love is not based on anything we do; it's based solely on him. He knows us completely, even more than we know ourselves, and he loves us completely. It is because of that love and with his power that we can put our sin to death and live in the newness of life he has given us (Ephesians 4:17–32; Colossians 3:1–17). It is because of the incredible reality of salvation and the promised inheritance we have in Christ that we are called to be holy as he is holy, and all with his empowerment (1 Peter 1).

When we come to God as beloved children, we can come with freedom and confidence. When we aren't working to earn love or acceptance but instead are believing the truth that we are loved, we are free to fully live out God's design. Incidentally, we also come to a deeper recognition of our sin and a stronger desire to put off the old and put on the new. Instead of duty or striving to earn favor, our obedience becomes joy and a pathway to abundant life in Christ. It becomes part of an abiding relationship in which we are truly at home.

Our human relationships can help conceptualize this. Years ago, I found myself seeking to earn my dad's acceptance or approval. God used that realization to show me that I was doing the same thing with him. When I stopped my efforts to obtain something from my dad, I realized I already had it. He loved me, approved of me, and accepted me fully. When I stopped seeking something I already had, I could fully experience my dad's love. I got to simply enjoy him for who he was, and I got to be who I was. It was freeing and filling. I got to just be my dad's daughter, and it was a joy. In my experience, that's what it's like with God too. When we relax and trust that we are accepted in the Beloved (see Ephesians 1:3–6), we can enjoy God for who he is. And we can enjoy the way God has designed us and the process of maturing in him. When founded on truth instead of fraught with performance, our relationship with God deepens. It rests on his character and what he has done, and in that, we are free to put our sins to death and to live the abundant life of Christ (Galatians 5:13–25).

God is the one who tends the branches and bears the fruit. We get to do the abiding! Abiding takes our effort (Philippians 2:12–13), which we'll talk about more in the next chapter. And yet, it is not about our strength, legalistic requirements, or sheer willpower. We simply cannot produce fruit apart from Christ. And if we are in him, fruit will result.

Abiding results in fruit because the more we are with God, the more we know him, and the more we will be like him. Fruit is the evidence of God's work in our lives (James 2:26; Matthew 7:16–20). When we are in him and he is in us, our lives reflect his character and nature and thereby bring him

glory (Matthew 5:14–16; 1 John 4:7–12). Again, human relationships are helpful. As mentioned in Chapter 5, the people
we spend the most time with tend to rub off on us. For example, do you notice yourself becoming more negative when
consistently around people with a dour view of life? Or more
hopeful when consistently around people with an optimistic
perspective? Have you ever met a friend's sibling and
instantly seen the similarities? My mom, sister, and I are often
told how similar we sound and how we have the same
mannerisms. Given the amount of abiding that I've done with
each of them, it's no surprise that I would reflect them.

This reflection piece is crucial. Part of Jesus' prayer for
future believers included "that the world may know that you
sent me and loved them even as you loved me" (John 17:23).
Abiding in Christ results in fruit that the world can see, which
points them to Jesus. Ephesians 3:7–12 indicates that it is also
a witness in the spiritual realm. The fruit of our lives is not
merely about personal holiness or even acts of kindness to
make life more pleasant for others. Neither is it only about us
enjoying God and experiencing true life in him. Abiding in
Christ, and the fruit that results, is about the world knowing
who God is. Abiding is about a genuine relationship with
God in which we become more like him, and we share in his
redemptive work by witnessing to the reality of who he is and
what he does. Abiding is about a relationship with him being
real in the deepest ways possible. In Christ, we are transformed and made new (2 Corinthians 5:17), and the evidence
of that touches every aspect of who we are, the ways we experience the world, and the ways the world experiences us.
Fruit is part of God's redemptive work in our lives and the
grander narrative of history.

And fruit means waiting. Plants produce in season, and
our lives often feel much the same. Generally, fruit does not
come quickly. It's not always immediately apparent what part
of the growth process we're even in. But God is not in a rush.

The process of sanctification is lifelong. We cannot force ourselves to bear fruit any more than a branch can. But we can yield to God's work of refining. We can intentionally abide in the vine for nourishment, waiting with eager anticipation for all God is doing.

CHAPTER 11

ABIDING—HOW DO WE DO IT?

W e've established that God is the source of security in our abiding. In Jesus' metaphor, the Father is the vinedresser, and he is the vine. We are the branches who are nourished, tended to, and pruned as we abide in him. Fruit is the result. We know the fruit is ultimately produced by God and that it requires effort from us. So, what is that effort? How do we go about abiding?

GOD'S WORD—JOHN 15:7

Abiding in Jesus is connected to allowing his words to dwell in us. John 15:7 uses the plural form of the Greek *rēma*, referring to that which has been said or taught.[1] This same root is in Hebrews 1:3, which says that Jesus "is the radiance of the glory of God and the exact imprint of his nature, and he upholds the universe by the word of his power." John 15:3, 20, and 25 use forms of the Greek word *logos*. That same

---

1. "G4487 - rēma - Strong's Greek Lexicon (esv)." Blue Letter Bible, accessed April 13, 2024, https://www.blueletterbible.org/lexicon/g4487/esv/mgnt/0-1/.

Greek root is used in John 1:1, referring to Jesus as the Word. *Logos* has a broad range of meanings, including that which is spoken, doctrine, instruction, reason, or that which embodies a concept or idea.[2] We see *logos* in John 17:17 when Jesus prays, "Sanctify them in the truth; your word is truth."

Jesus' words are not merely the red letters in the Gospels. The truth of who Jesus is and the reality of all he said and did are core. Hebrews 1:1–2 says, "Long ago, at many times and in many ways, God spoke to our fathers by the prophets, but in these last days he has spoken to us by his Son, whom he appointed the heir of all things, through whom also he created the world." Jesus tangibly shows us who God is.

In John 16, Jesus talks about the Holy Spirit's role in declaring more to the disciples; in fact, the entire chapter gives a wonderful depiction of how Father, Son, and Holy Spirit function together. He said it was to the disciples' advantage that he left so the Helper could come (v. 7) and that the Holy Spirit would "guide you into all the truth" (v. 13). First Corinthians 2:6–16 gives an illustration of how the Holy Spirit gives us an understanding of spiritual matters.

The disciples were to let all that Jesus had said and done while with them dwell in them, but they were not to stop there. To know Jesus is to know God, and that involves knowing all about God. The entire Bible points to Jesus and God's redemptive plan for humanity. Jesus did not come onto the scene at his birth. As God the Son, he has always existed. Second Timothy 3:16–17 tells us that "All Scripture is breathed out by God and profitable for teaching, for reproof, for correction, and for training in righteousness, that the man of God may be complete, equipped for every good work."

---

2. "G3056 - logos - Strong's Greek Lexicon (esv)." Blue Letter Bible, accessed October 27, 2024, https://www.blueletterbible.org/lexicon/g3056/esv/mgnt/0-1/.

The entirety of the Bible matters. As I've mentioned before, and as is hopefully evident by the fact that we're spending so much time examining Scripture, the most practical way for Jesus' words to dwell in us is Bible study. We need to know who God is, what he does, who we are, and how he calls us to be. This is something we need to do on our own and with others (Colossians 3:16). We learn from one another and help each other avoid misinterpretation and error. We also help each other "be doers of the word, and not hearers only" (James 1:22). God's Word does not truly dwell in us unless we allow it to shape our hearts, minds, and actions.

We need teachers too. Ephesians 4:11–12 says, "And he gave the apostles, the prophets, the evangelists, the shepherds and teachers, to equip the saints for the work of ministry, for building up the body of Christ." Paul instructed Timothy, "What you have heard from me in the presence of many witnesses entrust to faithful men, who will be able to teach others also" (2 Timothy 2:2). God has given us gifted teachers who know how to rightly handle the Word (2 Timothy 2:15) and convey it to others. The primary place for this is our local church (Titus 1:5–9; 1 Peter 5:1–5). Note that listening to gifted teachers is not a way to outsource your time with God in his Word. Teachers are helpful guides, but they cannot have a personal relationship with God on our behalf. We need to study the Bible for ourselves and avail ourselves of gifted teachers.

It is important to test our personal beliefs and any teachings we might hear against what the Bible says (Acts 17:11; 2 Timothy 4:2–5). And, of course, we need to employ good study habits to know what the Bible says. This includes things like making sure we're paying attention to context and being mindful in our exegesis. It also includes paying attention to the entirety of the Bible, not just our favorite portions (Acts 20:27; 2 Timothy 3:16–17). I've personally found Jen

Wilkin—author and Bible teacher—to be a helpful teacher on how to go about studying the Bible well.[3] One thing she mentions is that repetitive reading is one of the best ways to know the Bible. The more we're familiar with a passage, the better understanding we have and the more we're able to notice the nuances and see the connections. You might have heard the term *biblical theology* as related to tracing specific themes throughout the Bible. Though written by a variety of authors across centuries, the Bible is a unified book, ultimately authored by God. Thus, we should expect it will all fit together. After having teachers tune me into certain themes (like the woman and the serpent and the role of deception, or the way the exodus repeats throughout the narrative) the more I've come to appreciate the depth and beauty of God's Word. And my appreciation just grows! Every time I notice a connection, my love for God and my awe of him deepen. It makes my abiding richer and more trusting. Bible study becomes somewhat of a treasure hunt as I eagerly wait for God to open my eyes and show me more. So, regularly come to God's Word, including familiar passages. We need reminders of what the Bible says to keep us grounded in truth. Plus, there's often more depth than we realize. The daily deposits you're making through regular reading will pay dividends.

In rightly understanding the Bible, Wilkin also points out the importance of having an understanding of basic theology and the historical Christian faith.[4] No theological system will encompass the truth about God, but confessional creeds that

---

3. You can learn more about Jen Wilkin and her resources at her website: https://www.jenwilkin.net/.

4. For a helpful discussion on the importance of understanding the biblical story, basic theology, and living it out, see the TGC Podcast episode "The Church is Essential for Discipleship" (April 18, 2024; https://www.youtube.com/watch?v=w2rMCbO-tP0&list=PLPwoFK1MBpm7JcubSQCRD5E5ri08-1ia2&index=1), which features a panel discussion among J.T. English, Kyle Worley, and Jen Wilkin recorded at The Gospel Coalition's 2023 conference.

have stood for centuries convey foundational truths that are undeniable. Having a basic understanding of things like the Trinity, Jesus' identity as fully God and fully man, and the nature of humanity, sin, and salvation is crucial. Systematic theology as related to the essentials of the Christian faith can provide guardrails for biblical interpretation. Keep in mind that we have access to the larger body of Christ, including our local teachers as well as many other reputable teachers. Plus, we have the witness of Christian history. These are useful resources for understanding the Bible well.

The Bible is a basis for loving God with our heart, mind, soul, and strength (Mark 12:28–34). Given the nature of God and his Word, we will never fully master it. But that's part of the joy; there is always something new to learn, always a new depth (Psalm 119:18). I love Paul's prayer for the Ephesians: "That according to the riches of his glory he may grant you to be strengthened with power through his Spirit in your inner being, so that Christ may dwell in your hearts through faith— that you, being rooted and grounded in love, may have strength to comprehend with all the saints what is the breadth and length and height and depth, and to know the love of Christ that surpasses knowledge, that you may be filled with all the fullness of God" (Ephesians 3:16–19). God's Word is key to understanding who he is, and when we know him, we love him. When we love him, we obey him. And this is all part of abiding. We may not see fruit immediately, but as God's Word gets into our minds and hearts, it can do its work, and we will see the evidence. So, we remain and wait with hopeful expectation.

TRANSFORMED PRAYER—JOHN 15:7

Did you catch what Jesus said would be the result of abiding in him and his words abiding in us? "Ask whatever you wish, and it will be done for you" (John 15:7). First, to state the obvious, this is not a promise that God does everything we want him to do. He is not a genie who grants wishes; he is the self-existent, sovereign God of the universe. So, what does Jesus mean? When God's words dwell in us, our minds and hearts are transformed. Bible study isn't merely an intellectual pursuit. What lingers in our minds shapes the way we engage in life. Jesus' words dwelling in us is part of how we are "transformed by the renewal of your mind" (Romans 12:2). Our desires begin to be conformed to his. We begin to be able to discern his will, and our hearts long for his will to be done. Allowing Jesus' words to dwell in us deepens our relationship with God and enriches our prayers. This is all part of a relationship with God, participation in his work, and fruitful abiding.

God's words are meant to affect not just our prayers, but every aspect of our lives. We allow his Word to reveal and examine our hearts (Hebrews 4:12–13), to sanctify us (John 17:17), and to guide us (Psalm 119:105). We abide in God's Word by allowing it to permeate our days and the very fabric of our hearts. In Deuteronomy 6:4–9 God commanded the Israelites,

> Hear, O Israel: The LORD our God, the LORD is one. You shall love the LORD your God with all your heart and with all your soul and with all your might. And these words that I command you today shall be on your heart. You shall teach them diligently to your children, and shall talk of them when you sit in your house, and when you walk by the way, and when you lie down, and when you rise. You shall bind them as a sign on your hand, and they shall be as frontlets between your eyes. You shall write them on the doorposts of your house and on your gates.

God's words were for children and adults, in times of activity and inactivity, all day and everywhere they went. In

Jeremiah 31:33 God said, "I will put my law within them, and I will write it on their hearts. And I will be their God, and they shall be my people." God's law would not be merely external; it would affect their hearts and be part of their very identity. Paul told the Colossians, "Let the word of Christ dwell in you richly, teaching and admonishing one another in all wisdom, singing psalms and hymns and spiritual songs, with thankfulness in your hearts to God" (v. 3:16). God's Word was to live in them and color how they lived in community.

The call to know God's Word and abide in it has been a call for all of God's people at all times. To abide in God, we must know him. That means we need to spend time with him —through his Word, through prayer, and in community with others who also know him. It's a never-ending, ever-deepening process. It's waiting. So, we abide and we wait expectantly, knowing he harvests good things in due season.

OBEDIENCE AND LOVING OTHERS—JOHN 15:9–12

John 15:9–12 is packed with encouraging truths. Notice that Jesus compares his love for the disciples to the Father's love for him—the eternal love that exists within the Trinity. That is just astounding! It is in *this* love that we abide. This is a love that will never end and never fail.

Jesus also connects obedience to abiding in his love. In modern culture, that might sound a bit off-putting, or perhaps too conditional as if we earn love through performance. But that isn't what Jesus is saying. He compares this, again, to his relationship with the Father. The Father did not start loving the Son when the Son took on human flesh and fulfilled the plan of salvation. Also, we know God loved us before we loved him (1 John 4:10, 19). Clearly, God's love is given, not earned. We dwell in the love of God as we live out who and how God has called us to be.

God is our Creator. So, it makes sense that living according to his ways is how we best experience his love. When we function according to his design for us, we dwell in the *agape* love he has for us. His ways are for our best, which means following him is how we experience his love best. When we love someone, we seek to please them. When we truly understand who God is, we want to live according to his ways because we want him to be honored and glorified. To claim that we love God and yet go against who he is and what he calls us to is to deceive ourselves. We still sin because we still have our sinful nature, and God is faithful to cleanse us when we do (1 John 1:5—2:6). But when we love God, our hearts are increasingly oriented to wanting to follow him. And the more we do, the more we experience the full relationship of love in him. The more we obey, the more we truly dwell in him.

Have you gathered how this is all connected with joy? Jesus tells his followers to abide in God's love through obedience so "that my joy may be in you, and that your joy may be full" (John 15:11). God desires fullness of joy for us. Jesus gives abundant life (John 10:10). Obedience isn't about drudgery or performance. It's about knowing God, knowing his love, and living in his truth. Yes, it's about holiness and about worshiping a holy, just, and mighty God whom we are also called to fear (Proverbs 1:7; Hebrews 12:28–29). But, as John writes, "Whoever confesses that Jesus is the Son of God, God abides in him, and he in God. So we have come to know and to believe the love that God has for us. God is love, and whoever abides in love abides in God, and God abides in him. By this is love perfected with us, so that we may have confidence for the day of judgment, because as he is so also are we in this world" (1 John 4:15–17). When we are restored to our Creator, we can live as we were intended. We can live with confidence knowing that Jesus has paid the penalty for our sins. We can also live in freedom, trusting that God's ways are best and that there is life in them. When we obey, we experience joy because we are living out a right relationship with God. It is in a right relationship with him that we experience true life, abundant life, and joyful life.

What are Jesus' commandments? These would encompass all that God has asked of us through his Word. Jesus gets even more specific here; his command is for us to love others as he has loved us (also see John 13:34–35). In short, it is to live as a reflection of God and a conduit of his love in the midst of a lost, broken, and hurting world. It is to demonstrate *agape* love to everyone we meet, especially in the body of believers (Galatians 6:10). We are to act like our Lord and be a tangible light and image of who God is (Matthew 5:14–16).

John repeats the themes of love, truth, and life often in his writings. But he is not the only New Testament writer to do so. Peter, of course, also heard these instructions from Jesus. After explaining the incredible realities of salvation, he wrote,

> Therefore, preparing your minds for action, and being sober-minded, set your hope fully on the grace that will be brought to you at the revelation of Jesus Christ. As obedient children, do not be conformed to the passions of your former ignorance, but as he who called you is holy, you also be holy in all your conduct … knowing that you were ransomed … with the precious blood of Christ, like that of a lamb without blemish or spot. He was foreknown before the foundation of the world but was made manifest in the last times for the sake of you who through him are believers in God, who raised him from the dead and gave him glory, so that your faith and hope are in God. Having purified your souls by your obedience to the truth for a sincere brotherly love, love one another earnestly from a pure heart, since you have been born again, not of perishable seed but of imperishable, through the living and abiding word of God.
>
> 1 PETER 1:13–15, 18–23

The incredible realities of salvation lead to obedience, and obedience involves loving one another. And God's Word abides. It's all connected: the truth of God, the love of God, our obedience to God, and our love of others. Truth and love and abiding—these cannot be disconnected (2 John 1:1–3; Ephesians 4:15). There is no love without truth; there is no truth apart from love. Both abide because God is eternal. We experience and express both as we abide in him.

ABIDING THAT LASTS—JOHN 15:15–17

Every time I read John 15:15–17, the truth of it becomes more meaningful. These verses also encapsulate so much of what we've talked about in our time together. They're too good to not recopy here. Jesus said, "No longer do I call you servants, for the servant does not know what his master is doing; but I have called you friends, for all that I have heard from my Father I have made known to you. You did not choose me, but I chose you and appointed you that you should go and bear fruit and that your fruit should abide, so that whatever you ask the Father in my name, he may give it to you. These things I command you, so that you will love one another."

God tells us what he's doing. He has made himself known to us, revealed the grander redemptive narrative, and invited us in! We know we are waiting for the culmination. But we know who God is, so we wait with eager anticipation. We know we are called to abide. In doing so, we have meaningful participation in God's work in the world. The fruit he bears in our lives is fruit that lasts. And it's not just about producing fruit as if it were a production factory. It's relationship! Jesus calls us friends; he chose us. He invites us to pray, knowing that our heavenly Father is trustworthy and is the giver of all good things (Luke 11:5–13; 18:1–8; James 1:16–18). He calls us to love one another in the same way he has loved us (John

13:34–35). In short, God invites us into that which is truly life (John 10:10). He invites us into fullness of relationship with himself. He invites us to become like him in character, to live out his good purposes for us, to be in real relationships with one another, and to experience a right relationship with him. He is bringing final restoration—when all will be as it should be. He is bringing completion. In our waiting, we have a fore-taste. And what a sweet foretaste it can be!

AFTERWORD: ABIDING AND ABUNDANCE

I don't think I'll ever get over the reality that God not only tells us the grander redemptive narrative but invites us to actively participate in his work. We wait on the edge of our seats for what God will do in our lives and our worlds, but not as passive observers on the sidelines. Instead, we are active participants. The things we've talked about—deepening relationship with God, knowing him through his Word, praying, being obedient, loving others, and being a light to the world—are central. These have been the regular habits of believers for millennia (Acts 2:42–47), and they'll always be important. These are the routine ways we abide in Christ, and they always bear fruit.

Waiting is part and parcel of life in this world. For me, one intense season of waiting has led to a different season of waiting. My dad has gone home to be with the Lord, meaning my family has entered something new. What will this mean for our relationships and traditions going forward? The story of organizational growth is still in process. Relationships have been restored such that they are stronger and more honest than before the whole thing began, and the organization is taking strides to ensure continued thriving. Yet I remain uncertain about my future. The book dream has obviously resulted in a book! But where will it lead? My church is expanding, which means greater opportunities for women's ministry. But I don't know what that will look like or how God will weave the pieces together. My passion for leadership and people continues to stir, seemingly increasing by the day. My life is ripe with potential and anticipation. So, I am waiting and exploring, looking eagerly to see God at work and setting my heart to follow him every step of the way. Because of what I now know about waiting—and abiding—I live in this in-between with bated breath, expectant for all God will do.

All of us will always be waiting on God for something. Waiting is not something to minimize or merely put up with. It isn't pointless endurance or wasted time. It's in our waiting that our longing for the Lord deepens, our trust in him grows, and our love for one another grows. As we engage with hope, grief, heartache, joy, unmet longing, putting self to death, all that this in-between life holds, we do so knowing "the Lord is not slow to fulfill his promise as some count slowness, but is patient toward you, not wishing that any should perish, but that all should reach repentance ... according to his promise we are waiting for new heavens and a new earth in which righteousness dwells" (2 Peter 3:9, 13). That day will come, and the interim matters greatly!

It matters as a corporate body and in the grander arc of redemptive history. But it also matters in your life, in your circumstances, and in your community today. You are not an indistinguishable branch among many (1 Corinthians 12:12–31). God knows you intimately (Psalm 139), and he has a plan for your life (Ephesians 2:10). The fact that you bear his image, the unique ways he has created you, the spiritual gifts he works in you, the circumstances with which he has entrusted you, it all matters. It's all part of your participation in his grander work. It's also part of experiencing joy in the

Lord. When we live out who he has called us to be, in the general sense of reflecting his holiness and obeying his commands as well as in our unique positions in the body of Christ and our communities, we experience abundant life—fullness of life. We enjoy God and are keenly attuned to his work. When we intentionally steward design and circumstance, we more effectively serve his kingdom purposes. When our eyes are fixed on the Lord and on what he's doing in our present reality, we wait with anticipation and confidence. We abide with vigor. We find rest. Plus, it's just a whole lot of fun!

Much has been and can be said about God's design for humanity, the ways he works uniquely in the lives of individuals, and what it means to live the abundant life in Christ. I'll leave those topics for another time—a parting gift of waiting.

In the meantime, keep meditating on the profound realities and joys of waiting and abiding. We cannot have abundant life—that which is truly life as our Creator intended it—apart from Christ. There is no future hope on which to anchor our present reality apart from the Lord. But in him, there is great purpose in our waiting and great fruit in our abiding. When we abide, we experience what Jesus prayed before his crucifixion, "that they may all be one, just as you, Father, are in me, and I in you, that they also may be in us, so that the world may believe that you have sent me ... I in them and you in me, that they may become perfectly one, so that the world may know that you sent me and loved them even as you loved me" (John 17:21, 23). In our abiding, we experience the relationship and unity that our God invites us into. In our unity and love of one another, we reflect him. This is all so the world may know. What better thing is there than this abiding relationship with the God of the universe and Creator of our souls? What better life is there than abiding in him and sharing in his work in the world even as we wait for the full completion of his redemptive plan?

Circumstances press on us with powerful force. Distractions abound. Yet, God remains steadfast, and he invites you—always—to abide in him. So, "Wait for the Lord; be strong, and let your heart take courage; wait for the Lord!" (Psalm 27:14).

APPENDIX: GRANDER
REDEMPTIVE ARC

The grander redemptive arc of history is a term I often equate with the overarching narrative of Scripture. If you're unfamiliar with the biblical narrative, here's a summary.

God created the earth and all that is in it, and it was very good. He created humanity in his image and with incredible purpose. Humans were intended to have a full relationship with God, community with one another, and meaningful work. They were to "be fruitful and multiply and fill the earth and subdue it, and have dominion over the fish of the sea and over the birds of the heavens and over every living thing that moves on the earth" (Genesis 1:28). But the first humans chose to distrust God. They chose death over life, and we have been living in a broken world ever since (Genesis 3).

Human relationship with God, with one another, and with the rest of creation was destroyed. But God promised rescue —a Savior who would bring restoration (Genesis 3:15). We know that Savior is Jesus Christ (John 14:6; Acts 4:12). The Old Testament primarily describes God creating a people group from whom the promised Savior (or *Messiah*, from a Hebrew word meaning *anointed one*; the Greek equivalent is

APPENDIX: GRANDER REDEMPTIVE ARC

Christ) would be born and God's interactions with that nation, showing them their need for a savior and pointing to the type of person that Savior would be. It is filled with promise and anticipation.

God chose Abraham to father those people and promised him, "I will make of you a great nation, and I will bless you and make your name great, so that you will be a blessing. I will bless those who bless you, and him who dishonors you I will curse, and in you all the families of the earth shall be blessed" (Genesis 12:2–3; also see Genesis 15:1–20). God miraculously caused Abraham's wife Sarah to conceive a child—Isaac (Genesis 17:1–27; 21:1–7). God confirmed the covenant he had made with Abraham to Isaac (Genesis 26:1–5) and then again to Isaac's son Jacob (Genesis 28:10–17). Jacob's name was changed to Israel (Genesis 32:22–32), and it is this descendant of Abraham from whom the nation of Israel, and the promised Savior, would come.

The Israelite people were enslaved in Egypt for four hundred years where they grew into a larger population. God rescued them from that slavery through Moses (Exodus 1—17). The story of the exodus echoes throughout the biblical narrative, pointing to God's spiritual rescue of his people. When the Israelites were freed, God made a covenant with them (Exodus 19—24). He told them, "You yourselves have seen what I did to the Egyptians, and how I bore you on eagles' wings and brought you to myself. Now therefore, if you will indeed obey my voice and keep my covenant, you shall be my treasured possession among all peoples, for all the earth is mine; and you shall be to me a kingdom of priests and a holy nation" (Exodus 19:4–6).

God gave them specific commands (known as the Mosaic covenant) regarding their worship of him as well as how they were to live together. The people were given instructions to build a tabernacle, where God's presence would symbolically dwell, and he set aside the line of Aaron, Moses' brother, to serve as priests (Exodus 25—31). The seat of God's presence was behind a veil that only the high priest could enter once per year. He gave the people instructions about making animal sacrifices as atonement for sin and as offerings of worship. This was a shadow of what was to come. A better, permanent sacrifice, and a better, permanent priest were needed (Hebrews 9).

The Israelites struggled to obey God (just as we do). After the first generation of Israelites refused to enter the Promised Land out of fear (Numbers 13—14), they wandered for forty years in the wilderness, proving they needed a better rescuer than Moses. The next generation, under the leadership of Joshua, entered the land and each tribe was given a specific portion. But they did not fully drive out the people of the land, and they continued to disobey God, proving they needed a better leader than Joshua. After Joshua's death, the nation experienced a pattern of turning to idols, God allowing their enemies to overtake them, them crying out to God, and God providing a judge to rescue them, only for the idolatry to begin again (Judges 2:16-23; 21:25), proving they needed a better judge.

The people eventually asked for a king (1 Samuel 8—12). But their first king, Saul, disobeyed God, and God rejected him (1 Samuel 13:8-23; 15:1-35). David became God's anointed (1 Samuel 16:7-13). However, he committed many moral failures, proving the people needed a better king. Despite his egregious failures (2 Samuel 11—12), David persistently sought the Lord (Psalm 51) and is known as "a man after [God's] heart" (1 Samuel 13:14; Acts 13:22). When he was first anointed, the Holy Spirit came upon him and remained with him for his entire life. David is the quin-tessential king, and God made a covenant with him that the coming Savior would descend from his royal line (2 Samuel 7:1-17).

After the reign of David's son Solomon, the kingdom split

in two—Judah and Israel (1 and 2 Kings; 1 and 2 Chronicles). Sin patterns continued. God faithfully sent prophets to warn his people and call them back to him. But the people persistently turned away, proving they needed a better prophet. Eventually, both Israel and Judah were overtaken by other nations. Even so, God promised to make a new covenant (Jeremiah 31:31–40; Ezekiel 34:11–31; 36:22–38). The promise of a Savior—for all nations—remained, even when God's chosen people faltered.

The New Testament finds the Israelite people (the Jews) living under Roman occupation. It also finds them ripe for the coming of the Savior. The Old Testament is replete with promises about who he would be and what he would do. It is also full of Christ-types—people or events that demonstrate what the Savior would be like. The New Testament book of Hebrews is an excellent study of how Jesus fulfills the Mosaic sacrificial system and ushers in a new covenant as the better rescuer, sacrifice, priest, leader, judge, king, and prophet because Jesus "is the image of the invisible God" (Colossians 1:15) in whom "the whole fullness of deity dwells bodily" (Colossians 2:9).

The New Testament describes the coming of the Savior— the promise fulfilled! God the Son took on human flesh, lived a fully human life without sin, died on the cross to make atonement for sin, and rose from the dead, thus proving his claims are true that he is God and that his sacrifice is sufficient (John 1:1–14; 3:16–18; 1 Corinthians 15:1–7; 2 Corinthians 5:17–21). All who put their trust in him are forgiven of their sins, adopted as children of God, and given the indwelling Holy Spirit who will never leave them (Ephesians 1:3–14; 2:1–10). They are restored to a relationship with God and given family in Christ (Ephesians 4). The brokenness of the world caused by human sin in the Garden of Eden finds its solution in Jesus. Reconciliation with God is possible. Reconciliation with others is possible. And a right relationship with creation is possible.

Jesus spent about forty days with his followers after his resurrection before ascending into heaven (Acts 1:1–11). He promised to return (John 14:1–6; Acts 1:6–7, 11). He also gave his followers a mission, saying: "But you will receive power when the Holy Spirit has come upon you, and you will be my witnesses in Jerusalem and in all Judea and Samaria, and to the end of the earth" (Acts 1:8). The Holy Spirit came upon this group of followers about ten days later, at Pentecost (Acts 2), and he indwells all who trust in Jesus (Romans 8:9–17; Ezekiel 36:26–27).

The family of believers is known as the church. The New Testament chronicles its early history, provides theological foundations, and gives instructions for how we are to live as the people of God. This includes instructions for life together as well as for being a light to the world. Jesus also told his followers, "All authority in heaven and on earth has been given to me. Go therefore and make disciples of all nations, baptizing them in the name of the Father and of the Son and of the Holy Spirit, teaching them to observe all that I have commanded you. And behold, I am with you always, to the end of the age" (Matthew 28:18–20). This is the primary mission of the church.

Much as the Old Testament held promise and anticipation, so does the New Testament. We see, of course, the promise of the Savior fulfilled. We also see that all is not yet fully restored, but that one day it will be (Revelation 21—22). We currently live in the in-between. Redemption has occurred, and yet final restoration awaits (1 Peter 1:3–12; 2 Peter 3:8–13). So, we wait, knowing that the God who created all that is, who allowed his creation to rebel against him, who provided a means of rescue by entering fully into his creation and bearing the cost himself, who draws people to himself, who invites them to participate in his redemptive work, and who promises to restore all things, will surely be faithful to fulfill his Word. He is the God who is with us in our waiting and who promises that one day "the dwelling place of God is with man. He will dwell with them, and they will be his people, and God himself will be with them as their God" (Revelation 21:3).

DISCUSSION GUIDE

I would love to hear your story and witness what God is doing in your waiting. Feel free to contact me via my website to share: www.gwen-sellers.com. But assuming you and I can't meet for coffee, and even if we can, invite some friends to process with you. Share your hearts, process honestly, and pray together. Have good snacks too—remember, the present is a foretaste of full deliciousness, so enjoy! The questions below might help prompt your conversations:

1. What comes to mind when you hear the word *wait*? Do you tend to see waiting as a good thing?
2. Share about an experience of waiting in your life. What was the situation? How did it turn out? What did you learn?
3. What do you think of when you hear the word *abide*? What does it mean to you to be "at home" with someone or to "dwell" with someone?
4. What methods do you use to intentionally remind yourself of God's past faithfulness?
5. What attributes of God are particularly meaningful to you?

6. What do you long for the most?
7. How do you discern God's direction in your life?
8. What challenges you most about obedience to God in this season of life?
9. What positive fruit have you experienced in obeying God?
10. Do you tend to see things in your life as training? What might adopting that perspective look like?
11. Where do you regularly see evidence of God at work in the world and in your life?
12. Share about your experiences with Bible study. What excites you in studying God's Word? What challenges you in Bible study? What tools help? What passages are especially meaningful to you?
13. Share about your experiences with prayer. Do you find it easy or difficult to pray? How have you seen God use prayer in your life?
14. Share about your experiences in community. How has community been a challenge? How has community helped you? In what ways do you engage in community? How can we foster communities of truth and love, authenticity and growth?
15. Did you resonate with any of the stories or illustrations in this book?
16. What portion(s) of this book was most impactful for you?

ACKNOWLEDGMENTS

As many authors say, a book is not completed alone. My gratitude is foremost expressed to the Lord. I remain in awe of all he has done and expectant for all he will do. That he would provide salvation, give us his indwelling Holy Spirit, and invite us into his work in the world astounds me. More pertinently to this book, his depth of personal care and the ways he has worked in the details—some of which I've shared here—leave me speechless. I have loved this journey, and it is only by his enabling that I've gotten here. He also has provided so many who have come alongside!

To my sister, Saraah Ries, my gratitude is beyond words. You are my biggest cheerleader. You were a voice of reason in the midst of the waiting that prompted this book; a persistent believer in, champion of, and encourager of bringing the book to fruition; my first reader; and my editor extraordinaire. Your generosity, wisdom, godly example, and love bless me deeply. It's a gift to share in this life, and in this book, with you. Thank you for seeing God at work, believing in dreams I didn't know I had, and eagerly jumping in.

To my mom, Susie Sellers, another thank you beyond words. You lived the experience with me, listened *ad nauseum*, spoke wisdom and truth, and gave so generously of your heart when you were in an intense period of waiting yourself. You came to that first women's event, always eager to support me. You believed in the book from the beginning, continually encouraging me to pursue the dreams God gave me. You even invested financially to remove any barriers.

Your editorial input into the book has made it better. Throughout my life, you have been an example of what it looks like to know and love God and to abide in Christ. Thank you for leaning into him, letting me see it, and sharing the depths of joy we can have in him. As we like to say, you love well. Thank you for being the best mom I could ask for.

To my dad, who is now enjoying the presence of the Lord, thank you for making me feel secure in your love, for demonstrating what it looks like to wait well, and for trusting in the Father.

To Scott Frickenstein, who coached me through my season of waiting and whom God used in such meaningful ways. I would not be here today without the space, encouragement, and insights you (and your students) gave. Thank you for being part of the journey.

To Wade Brown and Jeannie Martin, whom God used similarly, thank you for stepping in at various stages of my waiting process with encouragement, insight, and a welcoming presence. God used each of you.

To Shari Hanson, who invited me to speak at her church and unknowingly prompted a devotional that eventually led to the writing of this book; thank you for being part of the journey and your continued encouragement.

To Pastor Josh Lindstrom and the elders at Woodmen Valley Chapel, who boldly led our congregation through a "year of sabbath." Thank you for listening to God's call and trusting him in obedience. Thank you, too, for your faithful teaching, which God so often uses to speak into my life.

To Pastor Kevin Feldotto, who called on me to be the women's ministry deacon for Woodmen Valley Chapel's Southwest family. Thank you for seeing me, for seeing what God was doing, and for inviting me in. Thank you for consistently loving me well in all the ways you pour into my life on a weekly basis.

To Tim and Sharon Burrows, who encouraged me—in this

book and women's ministry—and affirmed God's call. Thank you for seeing God at work and for all your prayers.

To Marcus Costantino, who convinced me I can and should write a book. Thank you for inviting me to the writers' conference and for sharing the passion God has given you. Thank you for walking me through the process and making the steps simple.

To Cristina Wright, my first professional editor. Thank you for nurturing this manuscript, your editorial insight and skill, and especially for sharing with me how God used it to touch you so that I would see this endeavor really is of him. Your partnership and participation are so appreciated.

To the entire team at Believers Book Services, thank you for all that you've put into making this book a reality.

To countless others who have prayed for me, waited with me, listened to me, spoken wisdom, encouraged me, shared their industry expertise, believed in the book dream from the beginning, and celebrated with me each step of the way, thank you! Community is featured prominently in this book because it matters, and I have been blessed with an especially good one.

Lastly, to you, dear reader, thank you for picking up this book and taking a chance on an invitation to abide. I pray you have been encouraged, and that God will bear much fruit in your life as you wait on him and abide in him.

ABOUT THE AUTHOR

Gwen is passionate for people to know and love God, be grounded in truth, and experience the fullness of life in Christ through the work of the Holy Spirit. She has tasted and seen his goodness, and she longs for others to do the same. Gwen holds a bachelor's degree in English from Whitworth University and a master's degree in counseling from Colorado Christian University. She works as an editor for a parachurch ministry, in which she enjoys regular exposure to God's Word. Among Gwen's greatest joys are her family, investing in the people and ministry of her local church, one-on-ones with just about anyone, exercise, blue sky, sunshine, and simply getting lost in thought. You can find her online at www.gwen-sellers.com.